Contemporary Discourse
in the Field of
BIOLOGY™

Cells

An Anthology of Current Thought

Edited by Jillian Lokere

The Rosen Publishing Group, Inc., New York

To Ting

Published in 2006 by The Rosen Publishing Group, Inc.
29 East 21st Street, New York, NY 10010

First Edition

Library of Congress Cataloging-in-Publication Data

Cells : an anthology of current thought / edited by Jillian Lokere.— 1st ed.
    p. cm. — (Contemporary discourse in the field of biology)
Includes index.
ISBN 1-4042-0398-2 (library binding)
1. Cytology—Juvenile literature.
I. Lokere, Jillian. II. Series.
QH582.5.C4583 2006
571.6—dc22

                                        2004028903

Manufactured in the United States of America

On the cover: Bottom right: A colored scanning electron micrograph (SEM) of paramecium protozoa. These protozoa are described as ciliate because many cilia (hairlike structures) cover them. Top: Digital cell. Far left: Digital cell. Bottom left: Austrian monk and botanist Gregor Johann Mendel (1822–1884).

CONTENTS

Introduction

Imagine yourself standing inside a huge factory, surrounded by intricate machines of all shapes and sizes. Your initial awe at the vast array of moving parts soon turns to curiosity as you try to understand just what each machine does, how it works in harmony with the others, and what might happen if a single part were to fail. If you were to shrink this factory to minuscule proportions—smaller than even the eye could see—you could be looking at a single cell, and your awe and curiosity would be what drives research in the field of cell biology.

Because cells are so tiny, generally spanning between 1 and 100 microns (1 micron = 1 millionth of a meter), it is easy to forget how important they are. Obvious reminders arise from diseases such as cancer or infections, when the functioning of the minifactories goes awry. Yet knowledge of cellular function can be applied to everything from bioweapons to new medical technology to an understanding of why a doctor might *not* want to prescribe antibiotic medications for a certain disease. Progress in biotechnology and medicine becomes so much more compelling with a clear grasp of cell biology.

Cell biologists study the structure, activities, and diseases of all kinds of cells. Because cells come in many shapes and sizes, it may seem as though a nerve cell and a skin cell, a plant cell and an animal cell, a bacterium and a fungal cell could not have very much in common. In truth, cells share many similar features, so experiments conducted using one kind of cell can often be applied to questions about other kinds of cells.

At the most basic level, all cells can be placed into one of two categories: prokaryotes or eukaryotes. Eukaryotic cells make up the human body, as well as other animals, fungi, and plants. A eukaryotic cell contains a nucleus, which houses its chromosomes, and a variety of organelles. These organelles allow the cell to produce energy, to metabolize food, to destroy unneeded molecules, to excrete waste products, to move, and to synthesize proteins and other molecules. The first section of this anthology explores these cellular structures and their functions. Through the eyes of leading researchers and scientists, you will discover how cells maintain their borders, how cells "communicate," and how some of the organelles function. This section will also take a close look at what defines a eukaryotic cell: the nucleus.

For all their complexity, the development of eukaryotic cells is believed to be completely dependent on their more primitive ancestors, the prokaryotes.

Prokaryotic cells, such as bacteria, are smaller and simpler than eukaryotic cells. Because prokaryotes lack a true nucleus and the complexities of eukaryotes, you might wonder how eukaryotic cells could not exist without prokaryotic cells. The second section examines the differences between the two classes of cells and peers deep into the past to discover how eukaryotic cells may have evolved through the capture of prokaryotic cells as "slaves."

As if to make up for this historical injustice, prokaryotes have come to be incredibly important for both human health and human disease. For example, bacteria that live in the human stomach are critical to the digestion process. These friendly bacteria help break down sugars and fats that would otherwise be lost. In return, they receive a constant supply of nutrients and a safe place to live. This symbiotic relationship between friendly bacteria and human beings isn't generally a topic of great interest—until the media report on a new outbreak of food-borne illness. It turns out that friendly bacteria can easily become dangerously infective pathogens! You will see why in the third section of this book. Bacteria cause other diseases and make deadly weapons as well. Who can forget anthrax or the black death? These are the other issues that the third section will explore.

A discussion of cells would not be complete without a look at one of their main enemies—the virus. Viruses measure between 20 and 250 nanometers (1 nanometer = 1 billionth of a meter) and contain their genetic information inside a geometrically precise protein shell, called a capsid. In order to replicate itself, a virus must find a way inside a host cell and take over the cell's machinery. Viruses are usually specific for a certain host, such as humans, birds, or bacteria. Viruses are well-known for causing diseases including influenza, the common cold, herpes, AIDS, smallpox, and Ebola.

However, viruses are not without their usefulness. In 1915, Félix d'Herelle, a British Canadian microbiologist, discovered viruses called bacteriophages that can only infect and kill bacteria. Bacteriophages are harmless to other kinds of cells. The idea of using phages to cure bacterial infections in humans has been around since that time, but the ease and efficacy of antibiotic medications supplanted research on phage treatments in the United States. However, a recent increase in the number of antibiotic-resistant, incurable bacterial infections has prompted scientists and physicians to revisit this treatment. A second area in which viruses may prove to be useful is the treatment of genetic diseases and cancer. These treatments require the patient to be infected with viruses that can deliver corrected genes to cells in which the genes are faulty, or that can kill cancer cells without harming normal cells.

The final section of the anthology will explore these topics. You will see how the tiny virus uses the cell's own molecules against it to gain entry through the plasma membrane and how it steals resources to replicate hundreds of times once inside. This section will also highlight some emerging medical treatments that use viruses. Although viral therapy is only used in clinical trials today, it has the potential to change dramatically medical treatments in the future.

The field of cell biology grows so rapidly each year that it would not be possible to capture each detail in one anthology. This collection will serve as a useful overview of cell biology, with special attention paid to practical and medical applications. Enjoy the journey of discovery! —*JL*

1 What Are Cells?

In order to carry out its many processes, a cell must first be separated from its environment. To do this, it surrounds itself with a flexible barrier called the plasma membrane. The plasma membrane, however, is more than just a barrier. The molecules within it, proteins and phospholipids, are in constant motion and flux. This article explores the structure of the plasma membrane and explains how it is neither a liquid nor a solid. We will also see how the plasma membrane controls what enters and exits the cell. Transport channels can actively shuttle molecules like glucose across the membrane, while ion pumps can create or maintain a concentration difference inside and out. Vesicles pop out from or fuse with the membrane, allowing excretion of waste and digestion of debris, dead cells, or invading bacteria. Within the membrane also lie receptors, without which cells could not communicate and our bodies would grind to a halt. More than a barrier, the membrane has a dynamic role in cellular life. —JL

"Border Control"
by James Kingsland
New Scientist, **July 15, 2000**

A living cell is like an ancient walled city buzzing with activity. It has its workshops, storehouses, administrative centre and streets teeming with traffic, but most importantly of all it is surrounded by a wall that encloses and defines it. This wall—the plasma membrane—is responsible for protecting the cell from its hazardous surroundings. Whereas walls were built to protect cities from armed invaders, the plasma membrane evolved to protect the cell from substances in its immediate environment such as toxic acids, alkalis, and ions. The evolution of an enclosing membrane was fundamental to the development of primitive life, just as the growth of the first cities was a milestone in human history. It provided a "reaction flask" in which to control and experiment with the chemicals of life in relatively stable conditions. And it allowed cells to maintain an internal environment that is ideal for keeping proteins stable and functioning.

Ever since, the membrane has prevented the escape of valuable products such as proteins, nucleic acids, and carbohydrates. But, like a city wall, it allows vital nutrients to pass inside through tightly guarded "gates" and waste products to be expelled, and as the only point of contact with the outside world, it can receive and transmit messages. In fact, by facilitating communication, the plasma membrane is the basis for all multicellular organization—allowing cells to cooperate in the building and maintenance of tissues and organs.

Just as the buildings within a city are protected by their own walls, discrete structures which perform particular functions within a cell—its organelles—are also surrounded by membranes with the same underlying structure as the plasma membrane. They are all composed of two sheets of phospholipid molecules arranged back-to-back. Most phospholipids have two tails that are hydrophobic—or "water-hating"—and a head that is hydrophilic—"water-loving." All the phospholipids in each sheet are aligned in the same direction, with their water-repellent tails weakly bonded to those of the other sheet to form a "lipid bilayer" about 5 millionths of a millimetre (5 nanometres) thick. In total, there are about a billion lipid molecules in the plasma membrane of a small animal cell, such as a red blood cell.

One of the remarkable things about the bilayer is that lipids are free to move rapidly in the plane of their own layer, making the structure a liquid crystal—neither solid nor liquid. This gives the membrane structural integrity but, at the same time great flexibility, allowing the cell to change its shape, expand and contract. The unique structure also allows the membrane to break and reassemble itself, which is vital during cell division and for forming small membrane-bound sacs called vesicles for importing and exporting large particles. To give some idea of the fluid nature of the plasma membrane, a single lipid molecule in a large bacterium can travel the entire length of the cell—about 3.5 thousandths of a millimetre for *Escherichia coli*—in a second.

Plasma membranes contain two other types of lipid: cholesterol and glycolipids. Cholesterol is an important constituent of all animal membranes as it prevents strong bonds forming between the lipid tails and so keeps the structure fluid. Glycolipids are mostly found in the outer "leaflet" of the bilayer, where they likely have a role in electrical insulation and inter-cell contact and recognition.

The membrane is studded with proteins, some of which are free-floating, others anchored to the cell's internal scaffolding, the cytoskeleton. Proteins account for about 50 percent of the membrane's mass, but there are around 50 lipid molecules for every protein molecule: the proteins are around 50 times bigger. The proteins act as receptors for transmitting information across the membrane, by binding to specific molecules in the environment and translating their signal into chemical messages inside the cell. They also act as channels and carriers allowing molecules in and out.

Membrane proteins come in two broad structural types. So-called transmembrane proteins extend from one side of the bilayer to the other. They achieve this feat by being amphiphilic—in common with phospholipids, they have both hydrophilic and hydrophobic parts. Their hydrophilic regions are exposed to water on either side of the bilayer, and their hydrophobic regions weakly bond with the tails of phospholipid molecules inside the bilayer. Often, they have regions of positive charge adjacent to the inner face of the membrane that firmly anchor them to the negatively charged phospholipid heads. Transmembrane proteins tend to be involved in ferrying substances across the membrane, or in mechanically linking the cytoskeleton to structures outside the cell, such as other cells or the mesh of fibrous proteins surrounding them.

Modes of Transport

By contrast, other proteins sit on the external or internal surface of the membrane, and these are often involved in cell signalling. They receive and transmit messages by binding to signalling molecules—a bit like throwing a switch controlling the chemical machinery of the cell or its neighbours.

What makes the plasma membrane so effective as a protective barrier in a watery environment is its hydrophobic interior. This allows the cell to maintain different concentrations of aqueous solutes inside and outside, and the same holds for membrane-bound organelles, such as mitochondria. Ions such as chloride, sodium, and potassium are unable to cross the bilayer unaided. Small polar molecules—molecules with an uneven distribution of charge—have some difficulty crossing it. But large polar molecules, such as sugars, amino acids and nucleotides, are incapable of breaching the closely knit, hydrophobic meshwork of the membrane interior. Water molecules on the other hand, despite being polar, are small enough to squeeze through.

In order to ingest nutrients, excrete waste products and regulate the concentrations of ions in their interiors, cells have evolved ways to usher selected substances across their membranes. Specialized transmembrane proteins transport ions and other water-soluble molecules. The importance of these proteins is testified by the discovery that almost one in five genes identified so far in *E. coli* codes for a protein involved in membrane transport. Each protein transports a particular kind of molecule. This was demonstrated in the 1950s, when biologists found that knocking out single genes in bacteria prevented them from transporting specific sugar molecules. In humans, several inherited diseases are caused by the inability of cell membranes to transport a specific molecule. Cystic fibrosis, the most common inherited disease in the developed world, is caused by a faulty membrane protein for transporting chloride ions and affects the cells of glands such as those that secrete mucus. As a result, extra-thick mucus is secreted that gums up intestinal glands, the pancreas and bronchi of the lungs.

There are two main classes of protein involved in transport: carrier proteins and channel proteins. The precise mechanism of transport remains unclear, but carriers are believed to bind to specific molecules on one side of the membrane, then transfer them across the bilayer by a series of reversible contortions, finally releasing them on the other side. They can be thought of as membrane-bound enzymes and the solutes they transport as their substrates.

By contrast, channel proteins form narrow hydrophilic pores through which small ions can rapidly diffuse from a high concentration on one side of the membrane to a lower concentration on the other. Diffusion is a passive process, so the cell doesn't expend any energy when ions pass through its channels. But only ions of a specific size and charge can negotiate a particular type of channel. Like enzymes, these proteins have binding sites for specific ions, making them highly selective. In addition, channels may open and close spontaneously, or they can be gated—meaning they will only open up under particular circumstances. Voltage-gated channels only open when a threshold potential difference across the membrane is reached; mechanically gated channels open in response to mechanical stress; and ligand-gated channels only open in the presence of particular ligands—molecules that bind to proteins, for example an ion or nucleotide inside the cell, or a signalling molecule outside, such as the neurotransmitter acetylcholine.

More than a million ions can diffuse through a single channel in a second—about a thousand times faster than transport by carrier protein. Combined with their hair-trigger responses to mechanical stress, ligands or changes in voltage, this extraordinary speed makes ion channels perfect for rapid reactions. Cells can build up large ion concentration differences across their membranes, effectively storing up potential energy like water building up behind a hydroelectric dam. This energy can be released in an instant when the ion channel floodgates open. The leaf-closing response of a mimosa plant is brought about by the sudden opening of ion channels, as is the ability of the single-celled *Paramecium* to change direction when it collides with an object. And every time you move a muscle you have ion channels in your motor nerves and muscle fibers to thank.

Whereas channel proteins merely facilitate diffusion, some carriers are coupled to a source of energy and actively pump solutes across the membrane—analogous to pumping water uphill. This "active transport" allows solutes to be moved against their electrochemical gradients. For example, ion pumps may move positively charged ions from an area where their concentration is low to an area where it is high, perhaps even from an area of overall negative charge to an area with net positive charge. They perform this trick either by splitting molecules of ATP, which is the cell's chemical fuel, or by harnessing the potential energy stored in the electrochemical gradient of another solute. Two of the best-known and most widespread ion pumps are the sodium-potassium pump, which plays a critical role in nearly all animal plasma membranes by helping cells maintain their volume, and the calcium pump which, among many other things, helps to regulate the contraction of muscle fibers.

A typical animal cell invests a hefty one-third of all its energy resources into fuelling its sodium-potassium pumps. In animal cells, the concentration of potassium ions (K^+) is kept between 10 and 30 times as high inside the cell as outside. The reverse is true of sodium ions (Na^+), and cells use this Na^+ concentration gradient to regulate their volume through osmosis. They also use it to drive the transport of sugars and amino acids into the cell. The Na^+/K^+ pump maintains these vital ion gradients by splitting ATP, and for every ATP molecule it splits the pump, expels three Na^+ ions from the cell, and admits two K^+ ions. Like all carrier proteins, the pump can be thought of as a membrane-bound enzyme, and since part of its job involves splitting ATP, it is referred to as an ATPase. Other membrane-bound ATPases function as calcium and hydrogen pumps.

Small, water-soluble organic molecules can also be shuttled across the membrane by specialized channel proteins called transporters. Some merely facilitate diffusion "downhill" from an area of high solute concentration to an area of lower concentration—known as passive transport—but others can actually pull solutes up their electrochemical gradient by using potential energy stored in another ion gradient. This is called secondary active transport, because it relies on ion pumps such as that described above to maintain the gradient.

A good example of the interplay between ion pumps and transporters can be seen in cells in the epithelial lining of the intestine. These cells perform the vital task of absorbing glucose from the gut on one of their faces and transferring it to the extracellular fluid on the other side—from where it passes into the bloodstream. On the side exposed to the gut's contents, glucose is carried across the membrane from a low concentration to a higher concentration by secondary active transport. In effect, glucose carriers use the passive diffusion of sodium from the gut into the cell to drive the transport of glucose. Meanwhile, on the other side of the cell, Na^+/K^+ ATPase pumps actively expel sodium from the cell to maintain this diffusion gradient. And as the concentration of glucose inside the cell rises, another kind of glucose carrier facilitates its diffusion into the extracellular fluid, and so into the bloodstream.

Even though biologists remain unsure precisely how carriers such as glucose transporters do their job, their handiwork is of enormous interest to drug designers. For example, it was recently found that a type of drug given to AIDS patients to stop HIV from replicating may have the unfortunate habit of blocking glucose transporters. The knock-on effect of this appears to be that patients taking these drugs, known as protease inhibitors, develop diabetes and have an unsightly redistribution of fatty tissue beneath their skin. Now that pharmacologists have some inkling about what causes these side-effects, they may be able to design drugs that are free of them.

Some molecules, such as proteins and nucleic acids, are too large to cross the membrane by any of the means described above. Instead, the membrane as a whole either allows part of the external medium to be brought into the cell, along with the molecules the cell needs (endocytosis), or part of the cytoplasm to be externalized (exocytosis). During endocytosis, the plasma membrane surrounds a portion of the external medium, rather like an amoeba engulfing its prey. The flexible membrane invaginates to form a hollow, then an almost-complete sphere. Finally, the membrane fuses and breaks to create a membrane-bound vesicle, which is drawn into the cell. Endocytosis may be triggered when a specific molecule, such as LDL cholesterol (the "bad" form of cholesterol), binds to a receptor on the outer surface of the plasma membrane.

Products earmarked for export from the cell, on the other hand, are packaged in vesicles which fuse with the plasma membrane, voiding their contents to the outside. This is how neurotransmitters such as serotonin—a brain chemical which helps to determine our mood—are released at the synapses which form the junctions between nerves.

Indeed, proteins called receptors that are embedded in the plasma membrane allow the activity of the billions of cells in a multicellular organism to be coordinated at every level. At the highest level, synaptic receptors for neurotransmitters such as serotonin and acetylcholine receive the long-distance messages being relayed through the nervous system. Hormone receptors perform an analogous role in the endocrine system, and receptors on the surface of lymphocytes and other immune cells mediate immune responses to invading organisms. But at the most fundamental level, receptors allow groups of specialised cells to cooperate with their neighbours in the formation and functioning of tissues and organs. They do this by interacting with the surface of other cells or by binding to molecules that other cells are secreting, then passing on these messages, for example to the cell nucleus where specific genes are activated or silenced accordingly.

Policing the Body

To take just one example, receptors in the plasma membrane of immune cells called T lymphocytes or T cells allow them to "police" the body, recognising and destroying cells that have been invaded by an infectious organism. Their receptors bind to so-called MHC molecules on the surface of other cells. The

MHC molecules present fragments of proteins or peptides. Healthy, uninfected cells present their own peptides, but infected cells also present peptides made by the invading organism. Whereas T cells do not normally respond to MHC molecules associated with "self" peptides, they trigger a full-scale immune response if their receptors encounter MHC molecules in association with foreign peptides.

If the T cells mistakenly react to self peptides, this results in an autoimmune disease such as arthritis or multiple sclerosis. In a similar vein, if T cells react to peptides that are foreign but otherwise harmless, the result is an allergic response, such as asthma or hayfever. Another, indirect consequence of our immune cell receptors' ability to recognise foreign peptides is the body's rejection of transplanted organs and tissues. Because MHC molecules vary enormously between individuals, the immune system recognises those that are not its own as foreign antigens.

Making it possible for immune cells to police our bodies is just one of the membrane's key roles. With the publication of the first draft of the human genome sequence, biologists now have the key that will unlock more and more of its secrets. The sequence of bases in individual genes indicates the sequence of amino acids in the proteins they encode, and around a fifth of the genome may code for transmembrane proteins. Once we know the amino acid sequence of receptors, ion channels and carrier proteins—and once we have learnt more about how these proteins fold up to create 3-D shapes—we can begin to solve the mystery of how they work. Over time we will learn to manipulate cells and treat disease with ever greater precision, by creating drugs tailor-made to interact with specific membrane proteins. We and our plasma membranes are truly living in exciting times.

The Ghosts of Human Red Blood Cells

More is known about the plasma membrane of human red blood cells than any other membrane. Biologists have been able to use them to discover a huge amount about the structure of the bilayer, the proteins it contains and its permeability to various substances. Thanks to red blood cells, the functions of many proteins, that are widespread in the plasma membrane of other cells, such as channels and proteins that link the membrane to the cytoskeleton, have been elucidated.

There are several reasons for these cells' popularity among biologists. They are available in large numbers (from blood banks) and they are easily separated from other blood cell types. And because red blood cells have no nucleus or internal organelles, researchers can be sure that they are only dealing with plasma membrane—in other cell types, only 5 percent of the cell's membranes are plasma membrane.

Empty red blood cell "ghosts" are prepared by placing cells in a solution with a lower salt concentration than that of the cytoplasm. Water floods into the cells through osmosis, making them swell up and burst, releasing their main non-membrane protein, haemoglobin, and other cell contents that could disrupt membrane experiments. While it is still broken, both faces of the membrane can be studied by exposing them to reagents. Such cells are known as "leaky ghosts." Alternatively, the cells can be allowed to seal up again, so that reagents can only reach the outer face of the membrane. A third option is to create "inside-out ghosts," in order to study the inner face in isolation.

Reprinted with permission from *New Scientist*.

Within the body, information needs to be passed from one cell to another constantly. For example, if you eat a sugary meal, cells in your pancreas can tell other body cells to absorb sugar from the bloodstream. Pancreatic cells do this by releasing a molecule called insulin. But how does insulin tell body cells to absorb sugar? How do cells communicate? In this article, Dr. John D. Scott, an associate investigator at the Howard Hughes Medical Institute and a senior scientist at the Vollum Institute at the Oregon Health Sciences University, and Dr. Tony Pawson, head of the program in molecular biology and cancer at the Samuel Lunenfeld Research Institute of Mount Sinai Hospital in Toronto, explain how the chemical messages sent by one cell are decoded and understood by another cell. First, protein receptors in the recipient cell's membrane specifically bind to the chemical message. Next, those receptors start a chain reaction of protein binding to

protein within the cytoplasm, much like Lego blocks clicking together. When the proper sequence of proteins are locked together, the cell is prompted to turn specific genes on or off, thereby "understanding" the message and responding to it in the proper way. —JL

"Cell Communication: The Inside Story"
by John D. Scott and Tony Pawson
Scientific American, June 2000

As anyone familiar with the party game "telephone" knows, when people try to pass a message from one individual to another in a line, they usually garble the words beyond recognition. It might seem surprising, then, that mere molecules inside our cells constantly enact their own version of telephone without distorting the relayed information in the least.

Actually, no one could survive without such precise signaling in cells. The body functions properly only because cells communicate with one another constantly. Pancreatic cells, for instance, release insulin to tell muscle cells to take up sugar from the blood for energy. Cells of the immune system instruct their cousins to attack invaders, and cells of the nervous system rapidly fire messages to and from the brain. Those messages elicit the right responses only because they are transmitted accurately far into a recipient cell and to the exact molecules able to carry out the directives.

But how do circuits within cells achieve this high-fidelity transmission? For a long time, biologists had only rudimentary explanations. In the past 15 years, though, they have made great progress in unlocking the code that cells use for their internal communications. The ongoing advances are suggesting radically new strategies for attacking diseases that are caused or exacerbated by faulty signaling in cells—among them cancer, diabetes, and disorders of the immune system.

Refining the Question

The earliest insights into information transfer in cells emerged in the late 1950s, when Edwin G. Krebs and Edmond H. Fischer of the University of Washington and the late Earl W. Sutherland, Jr., of Vanderbilt University identified the first known signal-relaying molecules in the cytoplasm (the material between the nucleus and a cell's outer membrane). All three received Nobel Prizes for their discoveries.

By the early 1980s, researchers had gathered many details of how signal transmission occurs. For instance, it usually begins after a messenger responsible for carrying information between cells (often a hormone) docks temporarily, in lock-and-key fashion, with a specific receptor on a recipient cell. Such receptors, the functional equivalent of antennae, are able to relay a messenger's command into a cell because they are physically connected to the cytoplasm. The typical receptor is a protein, a folded chain of amino acids. It includes at least three domains: an external docking region for a hormone or other messenger, a component that spans the cell's outer membrane, and a "tail" that extends a distance into the cytoplasm. When a messenger binds to the external site, this linkage induces a change in the shape of the cytoplasmic tail, thereby facilitating the tail's interaction with one or more information-relaying molecules in the cytoplasm. These interactions in turn initiate cascades of further intracellular signaling.

Yet no one had a good explanation for how communiqués reached their destinations without being diverted along the way. At that time, cells were viewed as balloon-like bags filled with a soupy cytoplasm containing floating proteins and organelles (membrane-bound compartments, such as the nucleus and mitochondria). It was hard to see how, in such an unstructured milieu, any given internal messenger molecule could consistently and quickly find exactly the right tag team needed to convey a directive to the laborers deep within the cell that could execute the order.

On the Importance of Lego Blocks

Today's fuller understanding grew in part from efforts to identify the first cytoplasmic proteins that are contacted by activated (messenger-bound) receptors in a large and important family: the receptor tyrosine kinases. These vital receptors transmit the commands of many hormones that regulate cellular replication, specialization, or metabolism. They are so named because they are kinases—enzymes that add phosphate groups to ("phosphorylate") selected amino acids in a protein chain. And, as Tony R. Hunter of the Salk Institute for Biological Studies in La Jolla, Calif., demonstrated, they specifically put phosphates onto the amino acid tyrosine.

In the 1980s, work by Joseph Schlessinger of New York University and others indicated that the binding of hormones to receptor tyrosine kinases at the cell surface causes the individual receptor molecules to cluster into pairs and to attach phosphates to the tyrosines on each other's cytoplasmic tails. In trying to figure out what happens next, one of us (Pawson) and his colleagues found that the altered receptors interact directly with proteins that contain a module they called an SH2 domain. The term "domain" or "module" refers to a relatively short sequence of about 100 amino acids that adopts a defined three-dimensional structure within a protein.

At the time, prevailing wisdom held that messages were transmitted within cells primarily through enzymatic reactions, in which one molecule alters a second without tightly binding to it and without itself being altered. Surprisingly, though, the phosphorylated receptors did not necessarily alter the chemistry of the SH2-containing proteins. Instead, many simply induced the SH2 domains to latch onto the phosphate-decorated tyrosines, as if the SH2 domains and the tyrosines were Lego blocks being snapped together.

By the mid-1990s, groups led by Pawson, Hidesaburo Hanafusa of the Rockefeller University and others had revealed that many of the proteins involved in internal communications consist of strings of modules, some of which serve primarily to connect one protein to another. At times, whole proteins in signaling pathways contain nothing but linker modules.

But how did those nonenzymatic modules contribute to swift and specific communication in cells? One answer is that they help enzymatic domains transmit information efficiently. When a protein that bears a linker also includes an enzymatic module, attachment of the linker region to another protein can position the enzymatic module where it most needs to be. For example, the act of binding can simultaneously bring the enzymatic region close to factors that switch it on and into immediate contact with the enzyme's intended target. In the case of certain SH2-containing proteins, the linker module may originally be folded around the enzymatic domain in a way that blocks the enzyme's activity. When the SH2 domain unfurls to engage an activated receptor, the move liberates the enzyme to work on its target.

Even when a full protein is formed from nothing but protein-binding modules, it can function as an indispensable adapter, akin to a power strip plugged into a single socket. One module in the adapter plugs into a developing signaling complex, and the other modules allow still more proteins to join the network. An important benefit of these molecular adapters is that they enable cells to make use of enzymes that otherwise might not fit into a particular signaling circuit.

Nonenzymatic modules can support communication in other ways, too. Certain molecules in signaling pathways feature a protein-binding module and a DNA-binding module that meshes with, or "recognizes," a specific sequence of DNA nucleotides in a gene. (Nucleotides are the building blocks of genes, which specify the amino acid sequences of proteins.) James E. Darnell, Jr., of Rockefeller showed that when one of these proteins attaches, through its linker module, to an activated receptor kinase, the interaction spurs the bound protein to detach, move to the nucleus and bind to a particular gene, thus inducing the synthesis of a protein. In this instance, the only enzyme in the signaling chain is the receptor itself; everything that happens after the receptor becomes activated occurs through proteins' recognition of other proteins or DNA.

As these various discoveries were being made, work in other areas demonstrated that the cytoplasm is not really amorphous after all. It is packed densely with organelles and proteins. Together such findings indicate that high-fidelity signaling within cells depends profoundly on the Lego-like interlocking of selected proteins through dedicated linker modules and adapter proteins. These complexes assure that enzymes or DNA-binding modules and their targets are brought together promptly and in the correct sequence as soon as a receptor at the cell surface is activated.

Fail-Safe Features Aid Specificity

Studies of receptor tyrosine kinases and of SH2 domains have also helped clarify how cells guarantee that only the right proteins combine to form any chosen signaling pathway. Soon after SH2 domains were identified, investigators realized that these modules are present in well over 100 separate proteins. What prevented different activated receptors from attracting the same SH2-containing proteins and thereby producing identical effects in cells? For the body to operate properly, it is crucial that diverse hormones and receptors produce distinct effects on cells. To achieve such specificity, receptors must engage somewhat different communication pathways.

The answer turns out to be quite simple. Every SH2 domain includes a region that fits snugly over a phosphate-bearing tyrosine (a phosphotyrosine). But each also includes a second region, which differs from one SH2 domain to another. That second region—as Lewis C. Cantley of Harvard University revealed—recognizes a particular sequence of three or so amino acids next to the phosphotyrosine. Hence, all SH2 domains can bind to phosphorylated tyrosine, but these modules vary in their preference for the adjacent amino acids in a receptor. The amino acids around the tyrosine thereby serve as a code to specify which version of the SH2 domain can attach to a given phosphotyrosine-bearing receptor. Because each SH2 domain is itself attached to a different enzymatic domain or linker module, this code also dictates which pathways will be activated downstream of the receptor. Other kinds of linker modules operate analogously.

A pathway activated by a protein called platelet-derived growth factor illustrates the principles we have described. This factor is often released after a blood vessel is injured. Its attachment to a unique receptor tyrosine kinase on a smooth muscle cell in the blood vessel wall causes such receptors to cluster and become phosphorylated on tyrosine. This change draws to the receptor a protein called Grb2, which consists of a specific SH2 domain flanked on either side by another linker domain, SH3. Grb2 is a classic adapter; it has no enzymatic power at all, but its SH3 domains (which like to bind to the amino acid proline) hook an enzyme-containing protein called Sos to the receptor. There Sos activates a membrane-associated protein known as Ras, which triggers a series of enzymatic events. These reactions ultimately stimulate proteins in the nucleus to activate genes that cause the cells to divide, an action that promotes wound healing.

The signaling networks headed by receptor tyrosine kinases seem to rely on relatively small adapter proteins. Analyses of communication circuits in nerve cells (neurons) of the brain show that some proteins in neuronal pathways have an incredibly large number of linker domains. These proteins are often called scaffolding molecules, as they permanently hold groups of signaling proteins together in one place. The existence of such scaffolds means that certain signaling networks are hardwired into cells. That hardwiring can enhance the speed and accuracy of information transfer.

Scaffolds Abound

One well-studied scaffolding protein goes by the name PSD-95. It operates primarily in neurons involved in learning. In nerve tissue, signals pass from one neuron to another at contact points called synapses. The first neuron releases a chemical messenger—a neurotransmitter—into a narrow cleft between the cells. Receptors on the second cell grab the neurotransmitter and then cause ion channels in the membrane to open. This influx of ions activates enzymes that are needed to propagate an electrical impulse. Once generated, the impulse travels down the axon, a long projection, to the axon's abundant tiny branches, inducing them to release more neurotransmitter. For the impulse to be produced, many components of the signaling system must jump into action virtually simultaneously.

Among the multiple linker modules in PSD-95 are three so-called PDZ domains. One binds to the cytoplasmic tail of the receptor for the neurotransmitter glutamate. A second grabs onto a membrane-spanning ion channel (which controls the inflow of potassium), and a third clasps proteins in the cytoplasm (as does an additional module in the scaffold). PSD-95 thus yokes together several signaling components at once, enabling them to coordinate their activities. The eye of a fruit fly also relies on a PDZ-containing scaffolding protein—InaD—for the efficient relay of visual information from the eye to the brain.

Yet another preformed signaling complex has been found only recently, in mammalian neurons. The core is a scaffolding protein named yotiao. As one of us (Scott) and his colleagues have shown, this molecule grasps a dual-purpose, membrane-spanning protein that is both a glutamate receptor and an ion channel. It also clasps a kinase that adds phosphate to, and thereby opens, the ion channel when the receptor is activated by glutamate. And it anchors a phosphatase, an enzyme that removes phosphates from proteins. The bound phosphatase closes the ion channel whenever glutamate is absent from the receptor. This elegant arrangement ensures that ions flow through the channel only when glutamate is docked with the receptor.

Kinases and phosphatases control most activities in cells. If one kinase activates a protein, some phosphatase will be charged with inactivating that protein, or vice versa. Yet human cells manufacture hundreds of different kinases and phosphatases. Scaffolding proteins, it appears, are a common strategy for preventing the wrong kinases and phosphatases from acting on a target; they facilitate the proper reactions by holding selected kinases and phosphatases near the precise proteins they are supposed to regulate.

Many Payoffs

From an evolutionary perspective, the advent of a modular signaling system would be very useful to cells. By mixing and matching existing modules, a cell can generate many molecules and combinations of molecules and can build an array of interconnected pathways without having to invent a huge repertoire of building blocks. What is more, when a new module does arise, its combination with existing modules can increase versatility tremendously— just as adding a new area code to a city turns already assigned phone numbers into entirely new ones for added customers.

For cell biologists, merely chipping away at the mystery of how cells carry out their myriad tasks is often reward enough for their efforts. But the new findings have a significance far beyond intellectual satisfaction.

The much publicized Human Genome Project will soon reveal the nucleotide sequence of every gene in the human body. To translate that information into improved understanding of human diseases, those of us who study the functioning of cells will have to discern the biological roles of any newly discovered genes. That is, we will need to find out what the corresponding proteins do and what happens when they are overproduced, underproduced, or made incorrectly.

We already know the amino acid sequences and the functions of many modules in signaling proteins. Hence, we have something of a key for determining whether the nucleotide sequence of a previously unknown gene codes for a signaling protein and, if it does, which molecules the protein interacts with. When we have enough of those interactions plotted, we may be able to draw a wiring diagram of every cell type in the body. Even with only a partial diagram, we may uncover ways to "rewire" cells when something goes wrong—halting aberrant signals or rerouting them to targets of our own choosing. We might, for instance, funnel proliferative commands in cancer cells into pathways that instruct the cells to kill themselves instead of dividing. By learning the language that cells use to speak to one another and to their internal "workers," we will be able to listen in on their conversations and, ideally, find ways to intervene when the communications go awry and cause disease. We may yet reduce "body language" to a precise science.

Simplified illustrations of the cell show the nucleus as a double-membrane-bound sac of chromosomes. Leading researchers in cell biology, including Dr. Tom Misteli, an investigator at the National Cancer Institute; Dr. David Spector, a professor at Cold Spring Harbor Laboratory; and Dr. Roel van Driel, a professor at the Swammerdam Institute for Life Sciences at the University of Amsterdam, have shown that the nucleus is actually complex and organized, containing discrete areas that carry out specific functions. Chromosomes themselves seem to contribute to this organization by clustering together in specific patterns, possibly by attaching to the inner nuclear membrane at certain points. One example of a functional compartment in the nucleus is the nucleolus, which contains ribosomal RNA subunits, proteins, and small nucleolar ribonucleoprotein particles (snoRNPs). The nucleolus serves as an assembly center for ribosomes. Now that scientists know that the nucleus is organized in a complex way, it is important for them to study nuclear processes in real time and in three dimensions inside the living nucleus. In this article, Dr. Lars Wieslander, a professor at Stockholm University, outlines this nuclear complexity and what it means for the development of new research tools and the thrust of future research. —JL

"The Cell Nucleus"
by Lars Wieslander
Experimental Cell Research, **March 2004**

Why is there a cell nucleus, or rather, what functional advantages and possibilities arose when cells with a nuclear envelope evolved? Prokaryotes do not have a nucleus, but carry out many of the processes that take place inside the nucleus in eukaryotic cells. Eukaryotes typically have a number of linear DNA molecules containing a large excess of non-coding sequences and they extensively use the coding information in a temporal and/or cell-specific fashion. Confining the separate pieces of the genome into a limited cellular space and organizing the DNA into chromatin, possibly in relation to the nuclear envelope, provides regulatory possibilities. Separation of transcription and RNA maturation from the active translation apparatus is probably a prerequisite for further regulatory possibilities. Recent insight into the dynamic and spatial arrangement of a number of "nuclear bodies" and of the molecular machines for transcription and RNA processing further underline that the cell nucleus is not simply a way of protecting the nuclear genome. The nucleus is more likely creating an optimized environment for performing regulated gene expression at the levels of chromatin, transcription, RNA processing and export of RNA. It is furthermore possible that regulation of cellular processes could be achieved by determining the nuclear versus cytoplasmic location of key molecules in a temporarily controlled fashion.

Nuclear Integrity

The nucleus is defined by the nuclear envelope, a double membrane that can be regarded as a specialized extension of the endoplasmic reticulum (ER). Regulated export from and import to the nucleus occur through large multiprotein nuclear pore complexes, NPCs. The outer nuclear membrane is continuous with the ER but the inner nuclear membrane contains a unique set of inner nuclear membrane proteins. A growing number of these proteins are being identified. The proteins usually interact with the nuclear lamina, the network of nuclear intermediate-filament proteins just inside the inner nuclear membrane. Many of the inner nuclear membrane proteins can also bind to chromatin. The interactions between the inner nuclear membrane proteins, the NPCs, the lamina, and the chromatin appear to be important for the integrity of the nuclear envelope and the entire nucleus. It is unknown how the nuclear envelope is assembled after mitosis. It is also not known how the NPCs assemble and how the inner nuclear membrane proteins reach their destination. Inside the nucleus, there are proteins that are able to form filaments. These include lamins, Tpr, and actin. It is still unclear if there is a protein scaffold throughout the nucleus that forms an underlying network of importance for the spatial organization of the nucleus and for the different nuclear processes.

Function, Chromatin Packaging, and Spatial Organization of the Chromosomes

The packaging and behavior of the chromosomes is central to the structure and function of the cell nucleus. The chromosomes play an important role in organizing the nuclear envelope around them after mitosis. A number of studies of interphase nuclei have analyzed the location of individual chromosomes, individual genes, centromeres, and telomeres in different types of cells. It is obvious that there is a non-random spatial organization of the chromosomes in cell nuclei. The patterns observed are however not easily interpreted in a generalized model. It is also unclear if and how the different functions are related to the spatial organization of the chromosomes. For example, in some cells but not in others, heterochromatic regions at centromeres and telomeres silence adjacent genes. Furthermore, centromeres and telomeres may cluster chromatin regions in the nucleus or anchor them at the nuclear envelope, and thereby influence the function of these chromosome regions. It is not known how the non-random spatial organization is brought about, but it appears as if chromatin packaging, positioning, and function are interdependent. For example, the nucleolus is likely to be formed as a consequence of rDNA transcription and ribosome biogenesis. It is also possible that transcriptionally active chromatin regions may be shielded from heterochromatic silencing by interactions directly or indirectly between components of the NPC and RNA export factors. Chromosome behavior in relation to mitosis and meiosis is an important aspect of the dynamic organization within the cell nucleus. The nuclear content and the organization of the chromatin vary in a cell cycle-specific way. First, the chromatin doubles during S phase and each pair of sister chromatids is kept together throughout G_2 phase until separation during anaphase in mitosis. Second, the formation of the kinetochore at the centromere of each chromosome is an essential assembly process in preparation for cell division. Third, starting in prophase, the chromatids condense into the maximally packaged metaphase chromosome. In sister chromatid cohesion and chromosome condensation, a family of chromosomal ATPases, the structural maintenance of chromosomes (SMC) family, plays important roles. These SMC proteins together with other proteins, form complexes, cohesin and condensin, that interact with the chromatin. How the different SMC complexes and other non-histone proteins function at the molecular level during cohesion, condensation, and separation of the chromosomes is still unclear.

Nuclear Compartments

A remarkable feature of the cell nucleus is that it is organized into many different compartments without the aid of separating membranes. The nuclear compartments have a unique composition of components, but often components are shared between different compartments. Some components appear to travel between several compartments in a defined temporal order. All these compartments, the nucleolus, PML bodies, Gems,

Cajal bodies, splicing speckles, paraspeckles, etc., are dynamic at several levels. First, they at least partly disassemble during mitosis and reform after mitosis. Second, their components come and go. Third, several of the compartments move around in the nucleus and their number, shape, and size varies.

If there are no membranes separating the different compartments of the cell nucleus, how do they form and how do they stay intact? Studies of many individual proteins in nuclei of living cells have shown that as a rule, the proteins are free to diffuse throughout almost the entire nucleus. These studies have also shown that proteins stay at different locations for different times, they have different residence times. A plausible explanation for the organization into dynamic compartments is that the different components of the cell nucleus have different binding affinities for each other. This could result in self-assembly of the compartments at steady state, without the need for any organizing protein network. The affinities can presumably be influenced by protein modifications, such as phosphorylations, thereby causing dynamic changes in the composition of the compartments.

The nucleolus is the most prominent nuclear compartment. The nucleolus was identified very early because it is so obvious in the light microscope without immunofluorescence staining. The nucleolus is one of the compartments whose protein composition has been analyzed by a combination of biochemical purification and mass spectrometry. It has a very complex composition of proteins and also various RNA species. Exciting studies are now going on that aim at understanding how the two ribosomal subunits are formed from a common pre-rRNA. We know the structure in detail of the mature ribosomal subunits from studies of prokaryotic ribosomes, but it is not known how the complex set of cleavages, molecular modifications and RNA protein interactions are coordinated during ribosome biogenesis. It seems that there must be a tight co-ordination between accessibility for processing proteins and snoRNPs and the gradual formation of the compact ribosomal subunits. A specific feature of the eukaryotic cell is that the ribosomes are made in the nucleus, but function in the cytoplasm. Most of the translation machinery is in fact present in the nucleus. Although it is possible that some form of translation can occur in the nucleus as part of surveillance of mRNA, it seems that mechanisms have evolved to prevent extensive translation in the nucleus.

The Need for Studying Nuclear Processes In Vivo

Individual nuclear processes, such as DNA replication, transcription, and pre-mRNA processing have been extensively studied in vitro. This has been a necessary step and will continue to be important in building up our knowledge about principles and molecular mechanisms. The fact that processes, such as splicing, usually are considerably slower in vitro than in vivo indicates that components and/or levels of molecular organization that is present inside the cell nucleus are missing in the vitro situation. In most in vivo studies, the read out is a recording of the final products. It is rare that the nuclear processes can be studied as they actually take place in the nucleus. This is particularly important to investigate because of the interplay between many different processes, but this is also where it gets really difficult. We need more methods for these types of analyses.

The study of splicing of pre-mRNA is a good example. It is striking that this complex nuclear process is rather efficient for pre-mRNA molecules introduced into nuclear extracts. This shows that the molecular splicing machine, the spliceosome, is flexible enough to handle an in vitro RNA transcript even if spatial relations between nuclear components and processes are disrupted. Nevertheless, it is quite likely that the biochemical picture from such experiments may fool us to some extent. To understand the splicing mechanism in vivo, it is necessary to analyze the recruitment and assembly of the more than hundred individual molecules involved in the splicing reaction, onto the growing pre-mRNA during transcription. This is so much more important because it has become increasingly obvious that the spliceosome is interacting with essentially all other molecular complexes needed for formation of an mRNA molecule, for example, the transcription elongation complex and the 3V'-processing machinery. We have also got a glimpse of a network of molecular interactions between molecular machines for pre-mRNA processing, surveillance and packaging, resulting in an exportable mRNA–protein complex. Furthermore, preparation of the mRNA for its cytoplasmic fate (efficient translation, specific localization or storage) depends on interactions between different processes in the nucleus.

In most cases, it is not fully understood how the different components of the various molecular machines are made and how they are stored and reused in the cell. The dynamics of specific components can be studied by in vivo microscopy and computational analyses. In the case of the spliceosomal components, we have come across surprises. Most of the small nuclear RNA protein particles of the spliceosome, the snRNPs, have to take a tour to the cytoplasm as part of their maturation. Several proteins are necessary for cytoplasmic maturation events and re-import of the snRNPs to the nucleus. One such protein is the SMN protein. For so far unknown reasons, insufficient amount of functional SMN protein results in motor neuron degeneration in the anterior horn of the spinal cord. The SMN protein is also present in the nucleus in specific nuclear bodies, so-called Gems and may also be involved in maturation of other RNPs, for example, snoRNPs. Back in the nucleus, the mature snRNPs cycle between storage in splicing speckles and spliceosome assembly at the active gene loci, but the molecular details of this shuttling are not known.

Nuclei in Specialized Cell

Specialized cell nuclei, such as in amphibian oocytes and in dipteran polytene cells, are exceptionally large and have specific chromosome organizations. Both of these circumstances permit experiments with a degree of three-dimensional resolution that is not possible in diploid cell nuclei. Comparing different kinds of cell nuclei shows that the same molecular components can be organized in morphologically different ways. For example, in mammalian cell nuclei, snRNPs are found in clusters of interchromatin granules. In amphibian oocytes, the snRNPs are present in large granules, B-snurposomes, and in polytene nuclei, no large or small granules have so far been observed. Studies of universal nuclear components and processes in the specialized cells have the potential to demonstrate aspects of nuclear processes that are most difficult to observe in diploid cell nuclei.

The Time Dimension

An important aspect of understanding the cell nucleus is the time dimension. It is essential, but not enough, to learn which molecules are present in the nucleus. It is not either enough to learn from immunofluorescence staining of fixed cells that a particular protein is preferentially present in a certain nuclear location. This is merely a snapshot of a most likely dynamic situation. Detailed analyses of the protein content of nuclear compartments after interfering with specific processes will give information about the relationship between function and dynamics. Using GFP tagged proteins and ways to attach proteins to specific DNA or RNA sequences, we are starting to get a view of the movements of individual proteins and whole nuclear compartments. These studies also give us estimates of the time factor, for example, that individual components in a large complex, such as a nuclear body, can move in and out of the complex with different kinetics. Furthermore, the kinetics of recruitment of factors during gene activation and transcription reveal how individual factors behave. This kind of knowledge makes a difference for how we think about the molecular mechanisms in the nucleus. A more complete understanding of the nuclear functions therefore requires that the time dimension is taken into account. We will definitely need systems and more sophisticated methods for in vivo studies of the kinetics of the processes that take place in the cell nucleus.

The tiny sperm drift around the giant egg like satellites surrounding Earth. A sperm enters the egg, and an embryo is formed. Although it seems like a simple process, some couples have an extremely hard time conceiving. Why is assisted reproductive technology often not successful in helping? In this article, you will read about the ideas of both Dr. Jonathan Van Blerkom, a professor at the University of Colorado, and Dr. David F. Albertini, a professor at Tufts University School of Medicine. The key seems to lie in the egg cell itself. Long before the sperm meets the egg, the egg must become organized and polarized in an orderly way. Although both scientists have different ideas about just how the egg manages to do this, they

do agree that an egg that shows disorganization in the cytoplasm or in the arrangement of the meiotic spindle is very unlikely to ever become a healthy baby. In truth, however, it is only by pregnancy itself that an egg can be decisively labeled "a good egg." —JL

"The Good Egg"
by Stephen S. Hall
Discover, May 2004

Shortly before 10:30 on a recent evening, with a nearly full moon luminous through mile-high air, Jonathan Van Blerkom climbed into his car, eased out of his driveway, and threaded his way through a quiet Denver neighborhood to check on the fate of some precious human eggs. They had been inseminated that morning, and some of them should be one-celled embryos by now. Van Blerkom's day had begun more than 16 hours earlier, but human development works the night shift, so Van Blerkom does too. Every evening, weekends included, he sets out on this five-minute drive to do one of the things he does best: look at very early embryos, only hours after fertilization, to decide if they are likely to become babies.

The embryos had been incubating all day in a small laboratory at Colorado Reproductive Endocrinology, a private fertility clinic where Van Blerkom, a professor at the University of Colorado, collaborates with in vitro fertilization doctors to help increase the chances that infertile couples can have children. He himself is not an "IVF doc." He is a scientist with a passionate, if not obsessive, curiosity about the biological factors that allow an egg to create a human. Ironically, that interest has also made him an expert in all the things that can go wrong with an egg and doom a pregnancy—even before it begins.

On this particular night, Van Blerkom dropped in to check on the status of eight eggs that were harvested that morning from a persistently infertile woman and soon afterward mixed with her husband's sperm. The woman had undergone several previous cycles of IVF at another clinic without a pregnancy, and Van Blerkom wasn't particularly hopeful about this round, either. "She's maybe a problem," he said in his low, urgent voice as he moved quickly about the lab.

Van Blerkom—dressed in blue jeans and a blue button-down shirt, a fringe of long graying hair sticking out like a worn-down but beloved brush—took great pains to keep the eggs warm during this nocturnal assessment. He turned on special heaters and waited about 15 minutes until the filtered air under a protective hood—where he would inspect the nascent embryos under a microscope—had reached 95 degrees Fahrenheit. Then he removed several small plastic dishes from the incubator and began to peruse the eggs.

For the better part of the past two decades, human embryologists have been staring at eggs and early embryos trying to decide which are "good" and which are not, which embryos seem most likely to yield a viable infant after implanting and which are destined to fail. These judgments have traditionally involved more art than science, as befits a procedure with an overall success rate of less than 34 percent. Van Blerkom has spent the last 25 years trying to inject scientific logic into these snap visual judgments, which last no more than 30 seconds.

Under the microscope, these eggs appeared like dark dots in a field of cellular clutter. "She has a couple fertilized," he remarked, removing the debris with a sharply pointed pipette. Then he moved to a second, more powerful Leica microscope attached to a video monitor. One by one, eight human egg cells, as big as the moon that Colorado night, loomed on the screen.

"This is at 10 hours after insemination," Van Blerkom said. "There, you can see the pronuclei." There on the screen was the huge, rotund universe of the female egg cell, its internal jelly, or cytoplasm, smooth and evenly grained, and there, just below the equator, two ghostly yolklike circles around the male and female DNA, mere mirages of genetic material, in close proximity, nearly nuzzling. Each gamete—egg and sperm—prepares its half packet of genetic material, known as the pronucleus, and one of the first organizational tasks of human development is to bring these two packets together. The glancing proximity of the male and female pronuclei on the screen represented the final stage of a daylong dance—a long latitudinal migration by the sperm's DNA to the site of the female pronucleus, so that the male and female chromosomes can "approach each other and melt into one," as a 19th-century embryologist poetically put it. That produces a complete set of human chromosomes and leads to the first division of the cell.

Even though the first several embryos looked smooth and even, Van Blerkom wasn't optimistic. "She doesn't have great stuff," he said. When asked how he could tell, he replied, "Just by looking at the quality of the cytoplasm in the unfertilized eggs. This is in pretty bad shape. These are not normal eggs.

"Look at this one," he continued. "This one has a lot of disorganization in the cytoplasm." And indeed, as more of the eggs filled the screen of the monitor—some fertilized, most not—the cells frequently had large vacuoles, or fluid-filled bubbles, in their interior. From experience, Van Blerkom knew that, although such eggs may become fertilized, they rarely produce a successful pregnancy. There is even a hint of evidence that normal-looking eggs from a woman who also has these abnormal eggs may fail to yield offspring.

"You look at these eggs, and you know they're telling a story," Van Blerkom said later. "But you only know bits of the story. If it were an abstract notion, who'd care? But around the world, thousands of people are looking down microscopes at thousands of eggs and asking, 'Should I keep this?' So life-or-death decisions for the one-celled embryo are made every day. My argument is, let's make those decisions based on biology."

For more than 20 years, Van Blerkom has been trying to understand the story that egg cells are telling, and although the tale is far from complete, some compelling new clues to early development have emerged. As both an academic studying the basic biology of mammalian development and as an IVF consultant with access to human egg cells and human embryos for research purposes, he is one of just a few scientists in a position to push a revolution in thinking about how—and whether—life begins. It involves the way an egg cell is built and how information positioned during that construction affects the fate of the embryo.

Scientific study of this phenomenon, known as polarity, could reveal how the fate of a human embryo may be shaped—and predicted—by extremely early biological events that predate conception by days, weeks, or even months. Surprising new research findings by Van Blerkom and others raise the paradoxical possibility that the viability of life may be determined long before fertilization.

The notion of polarity is quite simple. If you imagine the female egg cell (and later, the fertilized egg) as a spherical planet with its own intrinsic biological geography, then certain characteristics of that cell—the location of protein molecules or RNA messages or biochemical traits like pH or even the internal connective structures called microtubules—will be more prominent in certain regions, like one hemisphere as opposed to the other, or near the surface rather than near the core. Polarity of this sort has been known for a long time in the embryological development of simple animals like frogs and fruit flies. For just as long, it was not thought to be relevant to development in mammals.

But in the past few years, prominent British embryologists have shown that polarity exerts tremendous influence on the early development of mouse embryos. And several biologists in this country are pushing the idea of polarity in human development to more extreme conclusions. They argue that the fate of an embryo depends on the way the egg organizes itself, and that polarity in the egg can ordain either a successful or failed pregnancy *before* conception. This has profound implications for our understanding of life's origins, for our understanding of why so many embryos spontaneously abort in the first few days after fertilization, and for our understanding of why some IVF procedures may subtly affect early development, with potential long-term health consequences.

Most of all, it means that the scientists who study human development are increasingly looking at deep time, at events that shape the human embryo well before fertilization. The momentum of research, said Van Blerkom, is pushing embryology back into the realm of cell biology, because the fate of the organism is so inextricably tied to the quality of one cell above all: the egg. "In mammals," he said, "these are things that are too important to be left to chance." And so they are built into the eggs.

Back in the 17th century, when British physician William Harvey made his famous observation "*ex ovo omnia*" ("from the egg, everything"), natural philosophers believed that human development derived entirely from the egg. The sperm, in size as well as in deed, was puny by comparison. The most recent research confers molecular respectability upon Harvey's old maxim. Contrary to the message of 20th-century genetics, the success of the embryo may have less to do with embryonic genes than with maternal proteins passed on by the mother, and less to do with the embryo's DNA than with the maternal dowry the egg brings to conception.

The basic time course of fertilization and early development has been known for decades. When a sperm cell meets an egg cell (the oocyte), it burrows through the thick outer rind surrounding the egg (the zona pellucida), enters the internal cytoplasm of the egg (the ooplasm), and locomotes its male DNA—half of the typical number of chromosomes—to the female half within about three to four hours. During this microscopic odyssey, the sperm undergoes tumultuous transformations, using some as-yet-unknown materials in the cytoplasm to build a "beacon" to find the female pronucleus, its head of DNA swelling some five times its original size and then later condensing into chromosomes at the end of the journey. "The cytoplasm," Van Blerkom said, "dictates what the sperm does."

Once the two packets of DNA meld into one complete set of 46 chromosomes, the one-celled embryo begins to cleave, or divide, becoming a two-celled embryo at around 22 to 28 hours after fertilization, four cells another day later, and eight cells around day three. Only then do the embryo's own genes fully kick into gear and begin to function. Because these cells are grouped in a loose, pebbly collection resembling a berry, this stage of the embryo is referred to as the morula (from the Latin for "little mulberry"). Around the fourth day, however, the 15-to-25-celled mulberry dramatically tightens and seals its connections with neighboring cells (a process called compaction) and begins pumping fluid into its internal cavity. Now known as a blastocyst, the embryo undergoes a dramatic division of cell fate, forming a distinct outer layer of cells and an equally distinct bulge of about 20 or 30 cells on the inside. The outer cells (the trophectoderm) become the placenta; the inner bulge of cells includes embryonic stem cells, destined to form the entire fetus. Usually by the sixth day after fertilization, the blastocyst will hatch out of the egg cell's still-resilient rind and attach to the uterus.

The intricacy with which an early embryo divides, compacts, hatches out of the zona pellucida, ingeniously secretes molecules that penetrate the cells lining the uterine wall in order to implant in the womb, and then recruits blood vessels to nourish the placenta and the developing fetus marks one of the most awe-inspiring metamorphoses in all of nature.

But here's the rub: It's horribly inefficient in humans.

Much more often than not, the process fails. Although the statistics on the failure rate of human fertilization are not entirely robust, given the biological and ethical delicacy of conducting research in this area, the numbers consistently suggest that, at minimum, two-thirds of all human eggs fertilized during normal conception either fail to implant at the end of the first week or later spontaneously abort. Some experts suggest that the numbers are even more dramatic. John Opitz, a professor of pediatrics, human genetics, and obstetrics and gynecology at the University of Utah, told the President's Council on Bioethics last September that preimplantation embryo loss is "enormous. Estimates range all the way from 60 percent to 80 percent of the very earliest stages, cleavage stages, for example, that are lost." Moreover, an estimated 31 percent of implanted embryos later miscarry, according to a 1988 *New England Journal of Medicine* study headed by Allen Wilcox of the National Institute of Environmental Health Sciences.

In some respects, less scientifically sophisticated cultures may have come to terms with this conundrum in the way they grappled with the knotty question of when life begins. The medieval etymology of the word *conception*, said Harvard biologist John Biggers, traces it to the Latin root *capio*, which means to grasp, take hold, or receive into the body. In 1615 an obscure writer named Cooke noted, "Conception is nothing else but the wombs receiuing and imbracing of the seede," suggesting that centuries-old notions of conception referred, perhaps wisely, to when an embryo survived its perilous first week and was "imbraced" by the womb.

Nonetheless, the high failure rate begs challenging ethical questions. If life begins at conception, as many believe, why are so many lives immediately taken? If, as some ethicists argue, nascent life must be protected, how do we assess the degree of moral entitlement due a nascent entity that fails to pass nature's own muster perhaps 80 percent of the time? And if the fate of an organism is indeed inscribed in the earliest biological inklings of an egg, does life begin with the gametes?

From a purely scientific, not to mention pragmatic, point of view, the main question is more straightforward: Why do so many embryos fail to grasp the womb? That question has bedeviled developmental biologists for decades, and more recently, it has vexed clinicians who practice assisted reproductive medicine. Studying early human development in the academic setting is extremely difficult, in part because of political constraints on embryo research in the United States, so a certain amount of our knowledge is limited to inferences from animal studies.

Nonetheless, it has become increasingly clear that the fate of an embryo may be cast in the ovarian follicles, where egg cells are built. "Much of the developmental biology and ability of the human embryo is determined even before it's fertilized," Van Blerkom said. "This all happens by the one-cell stage, which is when the fate of the embryo is determined."

Such thinking upends long-held assumptions in the world of biology. Mammalian development was once thought to be essentially different from embryological development in fruit flies, frogs, worms, and other laboratory organisms, where well-defined polarities in the egg—higher concentrations of a protein in one part of the egg than in another, for example—ordained such fundamental aspects of body plan as head and tail, or back and belly. Mammals seemed exempt from these rules for building a body. In the mouse, it had been shown in the 1970s and 1980s that if you split an embryo at the two-cell stage, each resulting cell had the ability to develop into a full organism. If the egg were indelibly etched with asymmetric information that unequivocally determines development, the argument went, how could two embryonic cells be separated and still produce whole, intact, normal individuals? "Animal experiments led to the conclusion that mammalian eggs do not have polarity, but I think that's a *huge* fallacy," said David Albertini, a developmental biologist at Tufts University in Boston. One possible answer, he added, is that mammalian embryos are similarly shaped by polarity but retain a certain developmental flexibility as well.

These days, as biologists like Van Blerkom, Albertini, and a superb school of British embryologists based in Oxford and Cambridge have started to look at the early embryo, they have begun to catalog a number of very early polarities that affect both the competence of the egg and the form of later embryonic development. The implications of polarity reverberate far beyond the confines of academia. For example, Van Blerkom and Albertini have a gentlemanly disagreement about recent research that may spill out into the public discourse soon because it raises the possibility that some popular IVF techniques might have subtle but long-term health implications for children conceived in a dish. Indeed, on the night that Van Blerkom inspected the fertilized eggs at the Denver clinic, he made this disagreement clear at one point by holding up a sharp micropipette for my benefit. He remarked over his shoulder, "This is what I use to take off the cells that David Albertini says I shouldn't take off."

And with that, he began prying away the granulosa cells clinging to the eggs, in order to get a better microscopic view of the nascent embryos to see if they were developing properly. Within three days or so,

The Sperm Cell

Polarity begins in the sex cells. The female egg cell is a huge biochemical universe unto itself, with a complex and sophisticated cytoplasm. The sperm cell, by contrast, is little more than DNA strapped to an outboard motor. Nonetheless, of the 15 percent of couples experiencing infertility problems, about half the trouble can be traced to the male, mostly in the genetic qualities of the sperm.

Immature sperm cells form during the fourth week of embryological development but remain unfinished until puberty. At that point, the male begins to churn out haploid sperm cells—that is, sex cells with half the normal complement of 46 chromosomes. Thus, when a sperm cell delivers its genetic cargo at fertilization, the one-celled egg again possesses the full 46 chromosomes. Sperm dysfunction can arise from the way these cells are built. The sperm has an acrosome (the head and sheath), a nucleus, and a tail. Sometimes a club-shaped profile on the head disturbs the proper construction of the tail. These tail abnormalities can include looping, folding, and fusion, all of which can result in reduced motility (ability to swim).

While assisted reproductive techniques such as intracytoplasmic sperm injection (ICSI)—which involves the direct injection of sperm into the egg cell—can overcome head or tail abnormalities in sperm, recent animal research suggests that fertility doctors must use these techniques with care. Abraham Kierszenbaum of the City University of New York Medical School has conducted experiments in mice showing that even normal-looking sperm from a mutant mouse "is likely to create infertile offspring." Hence, selection of donor sperm, he said, cannot be based on appearance alone.

Biologist Jonathan Van Blerkom of the University of Colorado published a paper in 1996 suggesting that some cases of male infertility derive from defects in a tiny structure in the sperm cell called the centrosome. When a sperm penetrates the egg, it unwraps the centrosome, an organelle that acts like a construction foreman overseeing the creation of microtubules in the cell. Sperm DNA uses these microscopic highways to find the female DNA and merge into a zygote. If a sperm has centrosome defects, Van Blerkom speculates, it can get inside the egg but then is destined to wander in the desert of the egg's cytoplasm, unable to find its way to the female's DNA. —*S.S.H.*

those denuded embryos would be implanted in a woman's womb.

While the debate over polarity is much more sophisticated these days, it is not entirely new. In the late 1930s and 1940s, Arthur Hertig, John Rock, and several colleagues did an experiment in human embryology that to this day remains without peer in terms of elegance, revelation, and chutzpah. Working at the time as a researcher at the Free Hospital for Women in Brookline, Massachusetts, Hertig persuaded eight women scheduled to have hysterectomies to record intimate details of their lives prior to the surgery to remove their wombs, including when they menstruated and had sex. Armed with such precise information, Hertig's research team found developing embryos in either the fallopian tubes or uteruses of the women and, adapting the headlight from an automobile to illuminate their work, took photographs of early, preimplantation human embryos. Not only were they able to estimate when fertilization had occurred and also plot the time course of early human development, they also made an astonishing discovery: Half the embryos were clearly abnormal. This was the first concrete hint that most human embryos fail during the first week of development. Among other things, the paper that Hertig and Rock published in 1954 contained some of the first micrograph images of a human embryo at the two-celled stage. Hertig expressed the hunch that one of those cells was destined to be placenta, the other the developing organism.

Throughout his distinguished career (he headed the department of pathology at Harvard Medical School for two decades), Hertig suspected that there was a very early commitment by embryonic cells to become either a fetus or the placenta. He continued to explore this idea after his retirement, when Harvard set him up in an animal laboratory in the central Massachusetts town of Southborough to continue embryological research in monkeys. In the mid-1960s, the lab hired a teenager from nearby Hudson for a summer job cleaning out animal cages, and Hertig filled the kid's ears with his theories. "I had no idea who this guy was," the teenager would later say. "But he took me under his wing, and by the end of the summer, the guy is teaching me about ovaries and eggs."

A print of that first micrograph of a two-celled human embryo is now framed and hangs on the wall above the desk in David Albertini's small, crowded office at Tufts University where, 30 years after he cleaned the monkey cages in Southborough, he conducts research trying to figure out how the fate of those two cells is determined. The search keeps leading back to the mother's eggs. "You can't produce a healthy human unless you produce a healthy egg," said Albertini. "What endows a healthy egg, and thus a healthy embryo?"

In some respects, a human egg takes a lifetime to mature. Each female possesses up to 2 million oocytes at the time of birth, but that number is winnowed down to about 250,000 by puberty. Roughly 400 of these unfinished oocytes will mature and be ovulated during a woman's reproductive years, although the quality of the finished eggs declines as she ages. The vast repository of egg cells remains shelved in the follicles until the brain sends a signal in the form of monthly bursts of hormones, which trigger the final maturation cycle. From that signal, it takes approximately 110 days for an egg to grow, mature, and finally be released from the follicle.

In the late 1980s, Albertini's group began to focus on a group of satellite cells that surround the oocyte as it begins to grow and mature in the follicle. As eggs develop, each one is surrounded by a herd of much smaller hangers-on. These are called granulosa cells, and under the microscope they look like grapes glued to a beach ball. Albertini and his colleagues noticed that the interaction between the oocyte and the cells surrounding it was not symmetrical; there were more cells—and, it would turn out, more molecular back-and-forth traffic between the egg and the granulosa cells—at certain regions on the egg.

"We proposed that these cells on the outside were imposing an asymmetry on the egg," Albertini said. The pattern, originally identified in rodents, has now been shown to be true of cows, rhesus monkeys, and as of three years ago, humans. "Almost all animals build an egg in the ovary and position molecules in the top and bottom. This is a highly conserved evolutionary mechanism to make sure that when the cell gets subdivided, the cells at the top will become the head, for example, and the cells in the back may become a gonad. So you basically have to lay that down in the egg. And then you're just carving up the pie. We've been the first to have evidence to support that in the mammal, though not in the human yet. And there is evidence in human eggs, from Van Blerkom and others, that molecules are partitioned."

Unlike Van Blerkom, who has regular access to human eggs and embryos through his IVF-related work, Albertini works primarily with mouse and primate cells. But his lab's animal studies have revealed that asymmetry in an immature egg is important to the development of an embryo.

Through a series of elaborate experiments with mice, Albertini and his colleagues at Tufts have shown that the small cells bunched around an egg cell in the follicles are not mere microscopic groupies. They form connections, known as gap junctions, that send tendrils much like plumbing lines into the egg. The plumbing analogy is apt because molecules flow into and out of the egg through these channels. The molecules are critical to normal development: When the genes for certain of these molecules are experimentally erased, the eggs made by female mice are invariably defective, and the errors fatally disrupt the normal choreography of egg maturation.

Moreover, Albertini's group is exploring whether these plumbing lines, which corkscrew into the outer rind of the egg, play a role in establishing one of the most important geographic landmarks in the life of an egg cell—an event, Albertini likes to say when lecturing medical students, that marks "one of the most important days in your life."

"When you build a big round cell," Albertini said, "where do you put its nucleus? In most animals, you anchor it to one side, and that sets up all sorts of polarity." This happens early in the maturation of an egg cell, he argued, and is shaped by the position of the cells surrounding the egg.

When an egg cell matures, it must reduce its complement of DNA by half. This parceling process, called meiosis, occurs twice in the egg cell—once during a woman's fetal development and a second time as the egg is released from the ovary. During the initial phase of meiosis, as a woman's egg cell reduces its number of chromosomes from the normal 46 to the 23 found in sex cells, it parks one expendable sack of halved DNA in a spot near the cell surface. This is called the first polar body, and it defines one of the earliest discernible landmarks in the developing egg. This so-called animal pole is where the primordial nucleus of the one-celled embryo is destined to form. Just prior to ovulation, as the egg begins its second round of meiosis, it creates a spiderweb trace of proteins called the spindle, which allows the chromosomes to separate properly and is critical to a successful pregnancy. Spindle defects are believed to be the leading cause of the chromosomal abnormalities that doom so many early embryos.

Albertini's group now suggests not only that these outside cells tell the egg where to locate the polar body—and, therefore, the nucleus and spindle—but also that their plumbing lines soften up the egg cell's rind in the opposite, or vegetal pole, to increase the odds that sperm will penetrate the hemisphere opposite the nucleus. "We were able to study, in human oocytes, where the chromosomes were in relation to the polar body," Albertini said. "If the egg is born with an animal and a vegetal pole, the polarity must have come from the ovary because that's where the egg is built. The somatic cells [those outside the egg] may impose that axis. There are more cells, more connections on one side of the egg than on the other. Basically, what we're finding is that the side the nucleus is on has little contact with outside cells, and the further you move from the nucleus, the more connections you see." He believes that this sets up the internal organization of the egg's cytoplasm.

In fact, Albertini has preliminary evidence suggesting that the communication between the egg cell and its surrounding granulosa cells rises and falls in a precise monthly cycle. Since the monthly spike of a follicle-stimulating hormone seems to dampen the information exchange, he is now exploring the possibility that each ovulatory cycle not only releases a mature oocyte but also uses the monthly burst of female hormone to adjust the compass of polarity in the eggs that are still growing and will be ovulated one, two, or three months later. "We can only extrapolate to humans, but in the mouse, our data show that the whole process [of egg maturation] takes 18 to 20 days, and we can detect this asymmetry by the second or third day of the process. In humans, as an extrapolation, I'd predict that it would emerge between day 10 and day 20 in a 100-day process prior to ovulation—three full reproductive cycles before that egg would be used." If this preliminary hint holds up, the implications for maternal health become significant. Well before a woman attempts to become pregnant, she may be exposed to environmental effects—diet, prescription drugs, alcohol, and various toxins—that could affect the construction of her eggs. "Do you remember what you were doing three months ago?" Albertini asked.

The Albertini research, while pushing the starting time earlier, joins an emerging body of research establishing the impact of polarity on embryological development. In 2001, Magdalena Zernicka-Goetz and her colleagues at the Wellcome/Cancer Research UK Institute at the University of Cambridge did a clever experiment in which they dissolved colored dyes in olive oil and then stained each of the cells of a two-celled mouse embryo a different color—one blue and the other pink. As the embryo developed, the cells of the inner cell mass and the developing organism were predominantly pink while the cells of the developing placenta were blue, suggesting that developmental fate may have been etched into these cells from the moment of their very first division. This was, in a sense, a possible molecular answer to the hunch about early mammalian fates voiced by Arthur Hertig of the two-celled embryo half a century earlier.

Embryology has come a long way since those black-and-white images by Hertig. Van Blerkom has, among many other things, elevated the biology of human conception to high art. His lab in Boulder is filled with spectacular pseudocolor images that are every bit as dramatic as the peaks of the Front Range, which practically begin at the door to his office. The images depict what might be called embryology in flagrante: micrographs of sperm cells, trailing accordion-like pleats of white zags as they streak across a vast blue ocean of ooplasm; a multihued blastocyst in the process of hatching out of the egg's zona pellucida; and egg cells with a fringe of glowing, fate-determining proteins, looking a bit like a solar eclipse inside a cell.

These are more than just pretty pictures. Ever since the 1970s, when he worked in England with the developmental biologist Martin Johnson, Van Blerkom has sought ways to analyze, and visualize, secret compartments and regions of the human egg that may offer clues to whether it is endowed with good fortune or bad. "So many embryos don't work in the human," he remarked one day, in the midst of a six-hour conversation. "Why do so many go wrong? How does it go wrong? And how can you use that information? All of this stuff is going to come back to polarity. Human eggs that don't develop normally may be an issue of polarity." Asymmetries and polarities in both the cytoplasm and nuclear organization, Van Blerkom discovered, begin to appear even before fertilization. "It's a huge cell!" Van Blerkom said. "It's a 100-micron cell. And we know there are different things going on in different parts of the cell. There's incredible shuttling within the cells. How does that happen?"

Like Albertini, Van Blerkom sensed that the most important information in the embryo was not confined to the nucleus but embedded in the cytoplasm. "If I've done anything in this field," he said, "it's to deemphasize the embryo and emphasize the egg cell. Our work has shown that it all begins with the oocyte, which can have subtle cytoplasmic defects that are actually very profound. But," he added hastily, "you have to be careful. It's like looking at canals on Mars. Unless you can show a consistent pattern [of polarity] and then an effect that is different as cells divide, it doesn't have meaning."

Van Blerkom had been seeing hints of polarity since the 1970s, but one of the major turning points occurred in 1996 when, by accident, his lab discovered that cells surrounding the developing egg—the same granulosa cells that had piqued Albertini's interest—possessed a receptor very similar to the leptin receptor. Leptin made front-page news when it was discovered in 1994 because the molecule appeared to regulate fat metabolism and obesity. What was it doing in egg cells?

The Colorado lab discovered that granulosa cells—the cells that surround maturing eggs in the ovarian follicles—were pumping out leptin and shipping it into the egg. What's more, the researchers showed that leptin is polarized in the egg in such a way that, after fertilization, the protein is allocated primarily to the cells that become the placenta, while it is virtually undetectable in the cells destined to become the fetus.

At first, many embryologists resisted the notion that leptin was segregated in certain parts of the egg and that this asymmetry had any significance for the fate of the embryo. "For a long time, no one believed it," Van Blerkom said. But mice in which the leptin gene has been erased are incapable of producing embryos—the fertilized eggs die almost immediately. And various experiments tracking leptin inside the mammalian egg clearly showed a more prominent distribution in one hemisphere than in the other. It is now believed that this protein acts as a delayed silencer; it hangs around in the egg and keeps certain genes from turning on in certain parts of the embryo until days after fertilization. Again, the appearance of a protein in a certain part of the egg cell may affect embryonic development or the formation of organs days and weeks later.

Lately Van Blerkom has been intrigued by another form of polarity: the way mitochondria, the cell's little power plants, migrate in the maturing egg cell. "It's kind of like a lava lamp," he says, "with these blobs of cytoplasmic elements moving up and down in the cell." Typically, mitochondria arrange themselves along the outer edge of the egg cell. But at certain points in the reproductive cycle, they migrate en masse toward the nucleus. Wherever they gather, mitochondria change the local chemical microenvironment: They cause a lower pH, and that small change, Van Blerkom believes, can affect the local activity of certain enzymes. "It's not a bag of cytoplasm," he said. "It's highly structured, and that structure is changing."

Finally, Van Blerkom has conducted extensive work on the internal structural organization of the human oocyte. First the oocyte constructs the scaffolding of connections known as microtubules, which allow molecules to move around inside the cell. Then, toward the end of fertilization, the egg provides a kind of highway that allows the sperm to make its final approach to the female pronucleus. "There's something in that cytoplasm that allows the sperm to know where it's going," he said. One of the compelling messages—and central paradoxes—to emerge from these studies of polarity is that even bad eggs can be fertilized to create an embryo, but only good eggs seem to create a successful pregnancy. The politics of embryo research, however, is one reason we don't know more about what distinguishes good eggs from bad. Federally funded research on human embryos, although sanctioned by a congressionally mandated national bioethics commission in 1975, has faced unrelenting opposition from right-to-life groups. In 1996, Congress banned NIH funding outright for any research in which an embryo is destroyed. Van Blerkom calls the issue of when life begins the "third rail" of developmental biology. "You can find whatever you want in the embryo to support any position you have on when life begins," he said. "A lot of people believe that life begins at conception.

But life also ends at conception or shortly thereafter—hours after, a day after, four or five days after. We don't know why that happens, and what's gone wrong. We'd like to know the answers to those questions," Van Blerkom said, "but we can't do those experiments."

If polarity and the forces that shape it play a determining role in the fate of a human egg, it's not difficult to see the implications for making babies, whether through assisted reproductive technologies or the old-fashioned way. It becomes a particularly nettlesome question because basic research of the sort done by Van Blerkom and Albertini has historically been adapted—snatched, really—for use in IVF clinics, often before all the biological ramifications are clear.

Indeed, this is where the polite disagreement between Albertini and Van Blerkom becomes a matter of intense public and medical interest. If you believe, for example, that granulosa cells and other very early features of ovarian ecology set up the polarities that ultimately determine the quality of a human egg, as Albertini does, then certain techniques widely used in IVF may be subtly perturbing the very mechanisms that eggs use to establish a plan to build an embryo and maximize the chances that it will develop properly. "We recognized in the 1980s that many culture techniques used by assisted reproduction were reducing the quality of those eggs," Albertini said. "My own skepticism has been growing that we therefore may be damaging things with what we're doing to these eggs prior to embryogenesis." Other researchers—notably Alan Handyside in England—have begun to express similar concerns.

Albertini cites a popular IVF technique known as intracytoplasmic sperm injection, or ICSI, in which sperm is injected by needle right into the middle of an egg cell. If his polarity research in mice is true for humans, with its suggestion that sperm are biased toward entering the egg at the opposite pole from the cell's nucleus for important reasons, then ICSI injections might subtly disrupt patterns of polarity in the egg. Moreover, ICSI requires the removal of the cells surrounding the egg; Albertini thinks that might deprive the egg and early embryo of important signals or alter the time course of fertilization. Several rare, so-called imprinting disorders, including Beckwith-Wiedemann syndrome, a form of gigantism, have been found in children produced by ICSI, although the extent and significance of these links is unclear. "Ten years ago, we wouldn't have thought about the polarity thing," said Albertini. "It wasn't even on the radar. But now we're looking at how we're making these babies." Albertini hastened to add, "I'm certainly a proponent of human-assisted reproductive medicine, but I'm concerned that we're rushing technologies before we're certain they're safe and effective."

Van Blerkom respects Albertini's research but expresses reservations about his clinical ruminations. "If there were really problems with manipulating eggs, you'd see it, and in fact you'd have seen it 10 or 15 years ago," said Van Blerkom. "In the literature, there are only 26 reported cases of imprinting-associated disorders with IVF, and that is out of 1.2 million IVF births." In some hands, he added, ICSI is now achieving fertilization rates of between 60 percent and 70 percent, even though the technique requires the removal of surrounding cells. "If these cells were so important," he said, "you shouldn't get such high pregnancy rates."

Albertini replied that there might be subtle health effects, such as early onset of adult diseases like diabetes and cancer, that won't appear until 15 or 20 years after IVF, and he pointed out that there is very little follow-up data on the health of children created through assisted reproductive medicine. Even Van Blerkom conceded that point. "There's no systematic, organized mechanism for follow-up," he said. "And the reason for that is that people don't want it."

It may seem like an arcane debate, but it has life-and-death ramifications every day, when IVF practitioners peer at egg cells through microscopes and try to predict the fate of the embryos they might become. IVF remains, at best, a hopeful art driven by the best of intentions and less than complete knowledge. About two weeks after he sorted through those eight human eggs late one moonlit night, Van Blerkom called to report, happily, that his initial hunch had been wrong.

"I've got good news," he announced. "She's pregnant." It was a particularly felicitous way of acknowledging that, until biology provides a better crystal ball, pregnancy remains the best—and perhaps only—way to find out if an egg is good.

Reprinted with permission from Stephen Hall.

Proteins take on three-dimensional shapes in a process called folding. When a protein misfolds, it is marked as defective by the addition of the small polypeptide ubiquitin and is sent to the proteasome for degradation. Even defective proteins inside membrane-bound organelles, such as the endoplasmic reticulum (ER), are not safe; they can be deported from their organelle and destroyed by the proteasome lurking in the cytoplasm. How this is done is not fully understood by scientists. In this article, Dr. Randy Schekman, a professor at the University of California–Berkeley, summarizes two professional papers by professors at Harvard Medical School. These papers detail groundbreaking research in the export of defective proteins from the ER. The first, by Dr. Hidde Ploegh and his group, shows that a previously unknown protein, which they call Derlin-1, plays a major role in the transport mechanism. The second, by Dr. Tom Rapoport and his group, reports that a second unknown protein, which they call VIMP, interacts with Derlin-1. Together, these two research papers constitute a leap in understanding of the process that shuttles defective proteins out of the ER and into the cytoplasm where they can be destroyed. —JL

"A Channel for Protein Waste"
by Randy Schekman
Nature, June 24, 2004

Cells go to great lengths to ensure that protein molecules fold properly and function in the correct cellular compartment. Mistakes are dealt with harshly: the offending proteins are destroyed. [In] this issue, Lilley and Ploegh[1] and Ye *et al.*[2] describe how they identified a molecule that helps redirect proteins out of one compartment, the endoplasmic reticulum, to the waste-disposal machinery.

At first glance, the process of weeding out unwanted proteins seems straightforward enough. An elaborate cellular machine, the proteasome, attacks misfolded proteins that have become tagged with a small polypeptide marker, called ubiquitin. This machine is driven by the cellular energy store, ATP.

For many years, this editing function was thought to target only proteins that are found in the body of the cell—the cytoplasm—and it was assumed that other degrading enzymes would deal with proteins in distinct compartments. But around a decade ago, converging lines of investigation highlighted a role for the proteasome in the degradation of proteins that misfold in the endoplasmic reticulum (ER),[3-5] a major site of protein synthesis and the first port of call for proteins that are destined for the cell surface or to be secreted. Thus, mutant glycoproteins are somehow regurgitated to the cytoplasm, where ubiquitin tagging promotes the recruitment of the proteasome to the surface of the ER. ATP then drives the ubiquitin-tagged protein into the clutches of the proteasome through the intervention of another protein, called p97 in mammals.[6] The net outcome is that damaged goods are reduced to peptides and glycans.

Certain viruses that seek to subvert the capacity of an immunologically competent cell to mount an antiviral defence have exploited this editing pathway. Proteins known as class I major histocompatibility complex (MHC) molecules are essential in alerting the immune system to the presence of viruses, but cytomegalovirus has evolved a devious means of diverting newly synthesized MHC molecules from this task. Two viral glycoproteins, US2 and US11, insert themselves into the ER membrane and interrupt the flow of class I molecules to the cell surface, redirecting them to an enzyme that is responsible for ubiquitination and thus into the jaws of the proteasome.[7]

On their way out of the ER, redirected MHC class I molecules are assumed to pass through the same portal that is used for the regurgitation of misfolded cellular proteins. But no such connection has been firmly established, nor is the identity of this portal known. One candidate for such a channel is Sec61, a protein that creates the pore through which secretory and membrane proteins become inserted into the ER during their biosynthesis. Numerous experiments have hinted that Sec61 molecules transiently interact with MHC class I molecules as they are diverted to the proteasome,[8] and that mutations in Sec61 retard the degradation of misfolded secretory proteins.[9,10]

Unfortunately, these experiments did not reveal a direct molecular contact between Sec61 and proteins being redirected out of the ER. Other genetic studies have identified other membrane proteins that participate in the degradation of misfolded secretory proteins.[11,12] But, until now, no evidence linked these molecules directly to the transport of proteins out of the ER.

The two reports in this issue,[1,2] highlight the role of a mammalian equivalent of the yeast Der1 protein—which is found in the ER membrane and is required for the degradation of certain misfolded glycoproteins[11]—in removing proteins from the ER. Lilley and Ploegh[1] used the cytomegalovirus US11 protein to probe the environment of MHC class I proteins as they are diverted from the ER. By using tagged forms of wild-type and non-functional US11, the authors could track molecules in the ER membrane. They found that several previously unknown proteins could be precipitated in a complex with wild-type, but not mutant, US11.

One subunit of this complex was one of several mammalian relatives of yeast Der1. Like its yeast counterpart, this mammalian protein, Derlin-1, is found in the ER membrane, with the protein's chain snaking back and forth across the membrane a possible four times. It binds to wild-type US11 and MHC, but the complex decomposes quickly unless the proteasome is chemically inhibited.

A crucial experiment, documenting the physiological importance of Derlin-1, came with the demonstration that a hybrid protein containing Derlin-1 and green fluorescent protein blocks the US11-dependent degradation of MHC molecules. Surprisingly, though, this hybrid does not interfere with the action of US2, the other cytomegalovirus protein that diverts MHC molecules from the ER. So, US11 and US2 have distinct mechanisms of action. An obvious possibility is that US2 acts through one of the other mammalian Derlin proteins. In uninfected cells, each Derlin might proofread a restricted cohort of molecules.

Meanwhile, Ye *et al.*[2] pursued a different path to discover the ER proteins involved in MHC degradation. Given an essential role for the ATP-driven molecule p97, the authors probed the ER membrane for a p97 receptor. Their efforts were rewarded with a complex of two proteins, one of which was Derlin-1 and one of which they named VIMP (which might be one of the other unknown proteins that Lilley and Ploegh found).

Derlin-1, VIMP, and p97 co-localize to the ER, and might constitute the complex to which US11 and MHC class I molecules are recruited to initiate the export event. Using a cell-free reaction that reproduces MHC export,[13] Ye *et al.* trapped an intermediate consisting of VIMP, Derlin-1, US11, ubiquitinated MHC class I protein and p97. The stable formation of this complex required functional US11.

Broadening their findings, Ye *et al.* Also found that when cells were treated with dithiothreitol, a reducing agent that causes misfolded proteins to be directed out of the ER, more newly synthesized proteins that were bound up with VIMP accumulated. And blocking Derlin-1 expression in nematode worms promoted a form of cellular stress referred to as the unfolded-protein response, consistent with a general problem in the disposal of misfolded proteins.

So these studies[1,2] highlight a role for the Derlin-1 protein, and possibly for other members of the gene family, in the selective extradition of undesirable proteins from the ER. It is probably not the only such channel, however; yeast with mutations in Der1 can still dispose of many mutant membrane proteins, for instance[14,15] (R. Hampton, personal communication). Cells clearly hold many more secrets about how they deal with malfunctioning parts.

End Notes

1. Lilley, B. N. & Ploegh, H. L. *Nature* **429**, 834–840 (2004).

2. Ye, Y., Shibata, Y., Yun, C., Ron, D. & Rapoport, T. A. *Nature* **429**, 841–847 (2004).

3. Sommer, T. & Jentsch, S. *Nature* **365**, 176–179 (1993).

4. Hiller, M. M., Finger, A., Schweiger, M. & Wolf, D. H. *Science* **273**, 1725–1728 (1996).

5. McCracken, A. A. & Brodsky, J. J. *Cell Biol.* **132**, 291–298 (1996).

6. Ye, Y., Meyer, H. H. & Rapoport, T. A. *Nature* **414**, 652–656 (2001).

7. Weirtz, E. J. *et al. Cell* **84**, 769–779 (1996).

8. Wiertz, E. J. *et al. Nature* **384**, 432–438 (1996).

9. Pilon, M., Schekman, R. & Römisch, K. *EMBO J.* **16**, 4540–4548 (1997).

10. Plemper, R. K., Bohmler, S., Bordallo, J., Sommer, T. & Wolf, D. H. *Nature* **388**, 891–895 (1997).

11. Knop, M., Finger, A., Braun, T., Hellmuth, K. & Wolf, D. H. *EMBO J.* **15**, 753–763 (1996).

12. Hampton, R., Gardner, R. G. & Rine, J. *Mol. Biol. Cell* **7**, 2029–2044 (1996).

13. Shamu, C. E., Story, C. M., Rapoport, T. A. & Ploegh, H. L. *J. Cell Biol.* **147**, 45–58 (1999).

14. Hill, K. & Cooper, A.A. *EMBO J.* **19**, 550–561 (2000).

15. Vashist, S. & Ng, D. T. *J. Cell Biol.* **165**, 41–52 (2004).

2 What Is the Difference Between Prokaryotic and Eukaryotic Cells?

There are two categories of cells: eukaryotes and prokaryotes. Prokaryotic cells are unicellular organisms, such as bacteria, that do not possess a true nucleus or membrane-bound organelles. All multicellular organisms are made up of eukaryotic cells, but how did they develop their trademark membrane-bound organelles? Dr. Christian de Duve, the 1974 Nobel Prize winner in Medicine and a professor emeritus at the University of Louvain in Belgium, explains it through a theory of evolution by enslavement. The atmosphere 2 billion years ago was rapidly changing from anaerobic (without oxygen) to aerobic (with oxygen). Most primitive cells would not have been able to deal with the toxic by-products of oxygen, such as hydrogen peroxide. A few lucky prokaryotic cells developed the ability to neutralize toxic oxygen-based molecules. These "detox" cells may have been engulfed by larger prokaryotic cells as a potential meal. Instead of lunch, the smaller "detox" cells *were instead enslaved, and they are probably the ancestors of modern peroxisomes. With the power to deal with oxygen well under control, the larger cells were able to thrive and multiply, giving rise to the eukaryotic cells we know today. —JL*

"The Birth of Complex Cells"
by Christian de Duve
Scientific American, April 1996

About 3.7 billion years ago the first living organisms appeared on the earth. They were small, single-celled microbes not very different from some present-day bacteria. Cells of this kind are classified as prokaryotes because they lack a nucleus (*karyon* in Greek), a distinct compartment for their genetic machinery. Prokaryotes turned out to be enormously successful. Thanks to their remarkable ability to evolve and adapt, they spawned a wide variety of species and invaded every habitat the world had to offer.

The living mantle of our planet would still be made exclusively of prokaryotes but for an extraordinary development that gave rise to a very different kind of cell, called a eukaryote because it possesses a true nucleus. (The prefix *eu* is derived from the Greek word meaning "good.") The consequences of this event were truly epoch-making. Today all multicellular organisms consist of eukaryotic cells, which are vastly more complex than prokaryotes. Without the emergence of eukaryotic cells, the whole variegated pageantry of plant and animal life would not exist, and no human would be around to enjoy that diversity and to penetrate its secrets.

Eukaryotic cells most likely evolved from prokaryotic ancestors. But how? That question has been difficult to address because no intermediates of this momentous transition have survived or left fossils to provide direct clues. One can view only the final eukaryotic product, something strikingly different from any prokaryotic cell. Yet the problem is no longer insoluble. With the tools of modern biology, researchers have uncovered revealing kinships among a number of eukaryotic and prokaryotic features, thus throwing light on the manner in which the former may have been derived from the latter.

Appreciation of this astonishing evolutionary journey requires a basic understanding of how the two fundamental cell types differ. Eukaryotic cells are much larger than prokaryotes (typically some 10,000 times in volume), and their repository of genetic information is far more organized. In prokaryotes the entire genetic archive consists of a single chromosome made of a circular string of DNA that is in direct contact with the rest of the cell. In eukaryotes, most DNA is contained in more highly structured chromosomes that are grouped within a well-defined central enclosure, the nucleus. The region surrounding the nucleus (the cytoplasm) is partitioned by membranes into an elaborate network of compartments that fulfill a host of functions. Skeletal elements within the cytoplasm provide eukaryotic cells with internal structural support. With the help of tiny molecular motors, these elements also enable the cells to shuffle their contents and to propel themselves from place to place.

Most eukaryotic cells further distinguish themselves from prokaryotes by having in their cytoplasm up to several thousand specialized structures, or organelles, about the size of a prokaryotic cell. The most important of such organelles are peroxisomes (which serve assorted metabolic functions), mitochondria (the power factories of cells) and, in algae and plant cells, plastids (the sites of photosynthesis). Indeed, with their many organelles and intricate internal structures, even single-celled eukaryotes, such as yeasts or amoebas, prove to be immensely complex organisms.

The organization of prokaryotic cells is much more rudimentary. Yet prokaryotes and eukaryotes are undeniably related. That much is clear from their many genetic similarities. It has even been possible to establish the approximate time when the eukaryotic branch of life's evolutionary tree began to detach from the prokaryotic trunk. This divergence started in the remote past, probably before three billion years ago. Subsequent events in the development of eukaryotes, which may have taken as long as one billion years or more, would still be shrouded in mystery were it not for an illuminating clue that has come from the analysis of the numerous organelles that reside in the cytoplasm.

A Fateful Meal

Biologists have long suspected that mitochondria and plastids descend from bacteria that were adopted by some ancestral host cell as endosymbionts (a word derived from Greek roots that means "living together inside"). This theory goes back more than a century. But the notion enjoyed little favor among mainstream biologists until it was revived in 1967 by Lynn Margulis, then at Boston University, who has since tirelessly championed it, at first against strong opposition. Her persuasiveness is no longer needed. Proofs of the bacterial origin of mitochondria and plastids are overwhelming.

The most convincing evidence is the presence within these organelles of a vestigial—but still functional—genetic system. That system includes DNA-based genes, the means to replicate this DNA, and all the molecular tools needed to construct protein molecules from their DNA-encoded blueprints. A number of properties clearly characterize this genetic apparatus as prokaryotelike and distinguish it from the main eukaryotic genetic system.

Endosymbiont adoption is often presented as resulting from some kind of encounter—aggressive predation, peaceful invasion, mutually beneficial association or merger—between two typical prokaryotes. But these descriptions are troubling because modern bacteria do not exhibit such behavior. Moreover, the joining of simple prokaryotes would leave many other characteristics of eukaryotic cells unaccounted for. There is a more straightforward explanation, which is directly suggested by nature itself—namely, that endosymbionts were originally taken up in the course of feeding by an unusually large host cell that had already acquired many properties now associated with eukaryotic cells.

Many modern eukaryotic cells—white blood cells, for example—entrap prokaryotes. As a rule, the ingested microorganisms are killed and broken down. Sometimes they escape destruction and go on to maim or kill their captors. On a rare occasion, both captor and victim survive in a state of mutual tolerance that can later turn into mutual assistance and, eventually, dependency. Mitochondria and plastids thus may have been a host cell's permanent guests.

If this surmise is true, it reveals a great deal about the earlier evolution of the host. The adoption of endosymbionts must have followed after some prokaryotic ancestor to eukaryotes evolved into a primitive phagocyte (from the Greek for "eating cell"), a cell capable of engulfing voluminous bodies, such as bacteria. And if this ancient cell was anything like modern phagocytes, it must have been much larger than its prey and surrounded by a flexible membrane able to envelop bulky extracellular objects. The pioneering phagocyte must also have had an internal network of compartments connected with the outer membrane and specialized in the processing of ingested materials. It would also have had an internal skeleton of sorts to provide it with structural support, and it probably contained the molecular machinery to flex the outer membrane and to move internal contents about.

The development of such cellular structures represents the essence of the prokaryote-eukaryote transition. The chief problem, then, is to devise a plausible explanation for the progressive construction of these features in a manner that can be accounted for by the operation of natural selection. Each small change in the cell must have improved its chance of surviving and reproducing (offered a selective advantage) so that the new trait would become increasingly widespread in the population.

Genesis of an Eating Cell

What forces might drive a primitive prokaryote to evolve in the direction of a modern eukaryotic cell? To address this question, I will make a few assumptions. First, I shall take it that the ancestral cell fed on the debris and discharges of other organisms; it was what biologists label a heterotroph. It therefore lived in surroundings that provided it with food. An interesting possibility is that it resided in mixed prokaryotic colonies of the kind that have fossilized into layered rocks called stromatolites. Living stromatolite colonies still exist; they are formed of layers of heterotrophs topped by photosynthetic organisms that multiply with the help of sunlight and supply the lower layers with food. The fossil record indicates that such colonies already existed more than 3.5 billion years ago.

A second hypothesis, a corollary of the first, is that the ancestral organism had to digest its food. I shall assume that it did so (like most modern heterotrophic prokaryotes) by means of secreted enzymes that degraded food outside the cell. That is, digestion occurred before ingestion.

A final supposition is that the organism had lost the ability to manufacture a cell wall, the rigid shell that surrounds most prokaryotes and provides them with structural support and protection against injury. Notwithstanding their fragility, free-living naked forms of this kind exist today, even in unfavorable surroundings. In the case under consideration, the stromatolite colony would have provided the ancient organism with excellent shelter.

Accepting these three assumptions, one can now visualize the ancestral organism as a flattened, flexible blob—almost protean in its ability to change shape—in intimate contact with its food. Such a cell would thrive and grow faster than its walled-in relatives. It need not, however, automatically respond to growth by dividing, as do most cells. An alternative behavior would be expansion and folding of the surrounding membrane, thus increasing the surface available for the intake of nutrients and the excretion of waste—limiting factors on the growth of any cell. The ability to create an extensively folded surface would allow the organism to expand far beyond the size of ordinary prokaryotes. Indeed, giant prokaryotes living today have a highly convoluted outer membrane, probably a prerequisite of their enormous girth. Thus, one eukaryotic property—large size—can be accounted for simply enough.

Natural selection is likely to favor expansion over division because deep folds would increase the cell's ability to obtain food by creating partially confined areas—narrow inlets along the rugged cellular coast—within which high concentrations of digestive enzymes would break down food more efficiently. Here is where a crucial development could have taken place: given the self-sealing propensity of biological membranes (which are like soap bubbles in this respect), no great leap of imagination is required to see how folds could split off to form intracellular sacs. Once such a process was initiated, as a more or less random side effect of membrane expansion, any genetic change that would promote its further development would be greatly favored by natural selection. The inlets would have turned into confined inland ponds, within which food would now be trapped together with the enzymes that digest it. From being extracellular, digestion would have become intracellular.

Cells capable of catching and processing food in this way would have gained enormously in their ability to exploit their environment, and the resulting boost to survival and reproductive potential would have been gigantic. Such cells would have acquired the fundamental features of phagocytosis: engulfment of extracellular objects by infoldings of the cell membrane (endocytosis), followed by the breakdown of the captured materials within intracellular digestive pockets (lysosomes). All that came after may be seen as evolutionary trimmings, important and useful but not essential. The primitive intracellular pockets gradually gave rise to many specialized subsections, forming what is known as the cytomembrane system, characteristic of all modern eukaryotic cells. Strong support for this model comes from the observation that many systems present in the cell membrane of prokaryotes are found in various parts of the eukaryotic cytomembrane system.

Interestingly, the genesis of the nucleus—the hallmark of eukaryotic cells—can also be accounted for, at least schematically, as resulting from the internalization of some of the cell's outer membrane. In prokaryotes, the circular DNA chromosome is attached to the cell membrane. Infolding of this particular patch of cell membrane could create an intracellular sac bearing the chromosome on its surface. That structure could have been the seed of the eukaryotic nucleus, which is surrounded by a double membrane formed from flattened parts of the intracellular membrane system that fuse into a spherical envelope.

The proposed scenario explains how a small prokaryote could have evolved into a giant cell displaying some of the main properties of eukaryotic cells, including a fenced-off nucleus, a vast network of internal membranes and the ability to catch food and digest it internally. Such progress could have taken place by a very large number of almost imperceptible steps, each of which enhanced the cell's autonomy and provided a selective advantage. But there was a condition. Having lost the support of a rigid outer wall, the cell needed inner props for its enlarging bulk.

Modern eukaryotic cells are reinforced by fibrous and tubular structures, often associated with tiny motor systems, that allow the cells to move around and power their internal traffic. No counterpart of the many proteins that make up these systems is found in prokaryotes. Thus, the development of the cytoskeletal system must have required a large number of authentic innovations. Nothing is known about these key evolutionary events, except that they most likely went together with cell enlargement and membrane expansion, often in pacesetting fashion.

At the end of this long road lay the primitive phagocyte: a cell efficiently organized to feed on bacteria, a mighty hunter no longer condemned to reside inside its food supply but free to roam the world and pursue its prey actively, a cell ready, when the time came, to become the host of endosymbionts.

Such cells, which still lacked mitochondria and some other key organelles characteristic of modern eukaryotes, would be expected to have invaded many niches and filled them with variously adapted progeny. Yet few if any descendants of such evolutionary lines have survived to the present day. A few unicellular eukaryotes devoid of mitochondria exist, but the possibility that their forebears once possessed mitochondria and lost them cannot be excluded. Thus, all eukaryotes may well have evolved from primitive phagocytes that incorporated the precursors to mitochondria. Whether more than one such adoption took place is still being debated, but the majority opinion is that mitochondria sprang from a single stock. It would appear that the acquisition of mitochondria either saved one eukaryotic lineage from elimination or conferred such a tremendous selective advantage on its beneficiaries as to drive almost all other eukaryotes to extinction. Why then were mitochondria so overwhelmingly important?

The Oxygen Holocaust

The primary function of mitochondria in cells today is the combustion of foodstuffs with oxygen to assemble the energy-rich molecule adenosine triphosphate (ATP). Life is vitally dependent on this process, which is the main purveyor of energy in the vast majority of oxygen-dependent (aerobic) organisms. Yet when the first cells appeared on the earth, there was no oxygen in the atmosphere. Free molecular oxygen is a product of life; it began to be generated when certain photosynthetic microorganisms, called cyanobacteria, appeared. These cells exploit the energy of sunlight to extract the hydrogen they need for self-construction from water molecules, leaving molecular oxygen as a by-product. Oxygen first entered the atmosphere in appreciable quantity some two billion years ago, progressively rising to reach a stable level about 1.5 billion years ago.

Before the appearance of atmospheric oxygen, all forms of life must have been adapted to an oxygen-free (anaerobic) environment. Presumably, like the obligatory anaerobes of today, they were extremely sensitive to oxygen. Within cells, oxygen readily generates several toxic chemical groups. These cellular poisons include the superoxide ion, the hydroxyl radical and hydrogen peroxide. As oxygen concentration rose two billion years ago, many early organisms probably fell victim to the "oxygen holocaust." Survivors included those cells that found refuge in some oxygen-free location or had developed other protection against oxygen toxicity.

These facts point to an attractive hypothesis. Perhaps the phagocytic forerunner of eukaryotes was anaerobic and was rescued from the oxygen crisis by the aerobic ancestors of mitochondria: cells that not only destroyed the dangerous oxygen (by converting it to innocuous water) but even turned it into a tremendously useful ally. This theory would neatly account for the apparent lifesaving effect of mitochondrial adoption and has enjoyed considerable favor.

Yet there is a problem with this idea. Adaptation to oxygen very likely took place gradually, starting with primitive systems of oxygen detoxification. A considerable amount of time must have been needed to reach the ultimate sophistication of modern mitochondria. How did anaerobic phagocytes survive during all the time it took for the ancestors of mitochondria to evolve?

A solution to this puzzle is suggested by the fact that eukaryotic cells contain other oxygen-utilizing organelles, as widely distributed throughout the plant and animal world as mitochondria much more primitive in structure and composition. These are the peroxisomes. Peroxisomes, like mitochondria, carry out a number of oxidizing metabolic reactions. Unlike mitochondria, however, they do not use the energy released by these reactions to assemble ATP but squander it as heat. In the process, they convert oxygen to hydrogen peroxide, but then they destroy this dangerous compound with an enzyme called catalase. Peroxisomes also contain an enzyme that removes the superoxide ion. They therefore qualify eminently as primary rescuers from oxygen toxicity.

I first made this argument in 1969, when peroxisomes were believed to be specialized parts of the cytomembrane system. I thus included peroxisomes within the general membrane expansion model I had proposed for the development of the primitive phagocyte. Afterward, experiments by the late Brian H. Poole and by Paul B. Lazarow, my associates at the Rockefeller University, conclusively demonstrated that peroxisomes are entirely unrelated to the cytomembrane system. Instead they acquire their proteins much as mitochondria and plastids do (by a process I will explain shortly). Hence, it seemed reasonable that all three organelles began as endosymbionts. So, in 1982, I revised my original proposal and suggested that peroxisomes might stem from primitive aerobic bacteria that were adopted before mitochondria. These early oxygen detoxifiers could have protected their host cells during all the time it took for the ancestors of mitochondria to reach the high efficiency they possessed when they were adopted.

So far researchers have obtained no solid evidence to support this hypothesis or, for that matter, to disprove it. Unlike mitochondria and plastids, peroxisomes do not contain the remnants of an independent genetic system. This observation nonetheless remains compatible with the theory that peroxisomes developed from an endosymbiont. Mitochondria and plastids have lost most of their original genes to the nucleus, and the older peroxisomes could have lost all their DNA by now.

Whichever way they were acquired, peroxisomes may well have allowed early eukaryotes to weather the oxygen crisis. Their ubiquitous distribution would thereby be explained. The tremendous gain in energy retrieval provided with the coupling of the formation of ATP to oxygen utilization would account for the subsequent adoption of mitochondria, organelles that have the additional advantage of keeping the oxygen in their surroundings at a much lower level than peroxisomes can maintain.

Why then did peroxisomes not disappear after mitochondria were in place? By the time eukaryotic cells acquired mitochondria, some peroxisomal activities (for instance, the metabolism of certain fatty acids) must have become so vital that these primitive organelles could not be eliminated by natural selection. Hence, peroxisomes and mitochondria are found together in most modern eukaryotic cells.

The other major organelles of endosymbiont origin are the plastids, whose main representatives are the chloroplasts, the green photosynthetic organelles of unicellular algae and multicellular plants. Plastids are derived from cyanobacteria, the prokaryotes responsible for the oxygen crisis. Their adoption as endosymbionts quite likely followed that of mitochondria. The selective advantages that favored the adoption of photosynthetic endosymbionts are obvious. Cells that had once needed a constant food supply henceforth thrived on nothing more than air, water, a few dissolved minerals, and light. In fact, there is evidence that eukaryotic cells acquired plastids at least three separate times, giving rise to green, red, and brown algae. Members of the first of these groups were later to form multicellular plants.

From Prisoner to Slave

What started as an uneasy truce soon turned into the progressive enslavement of the captured endosymbiont prisoners by their phagocytic hosts. This subjugation was achieved by the piecemeal transfer of most of the endosymbionts' genes to the host cell's nucleus. In itself, the uptake of genes by the nucleus is not particularly extraordinary. When foreign genes are introduced into the cytoplasm of a cell (as in some bioengineering experiments), they can readily home to the nucleus and function there. That is, they replicate during cell division and can serve as the master templates for the production of proteins. But the migration of genes from endosymbionts to the nucleus is remarkable because it seems to have raised more difficulties than it solved. Once this transfer occurred, the proteins encoded by these genes began to be manufactured in the cytoplasm of the host cell (where the products of all nuclear genes are constructed). These molecules had then to migrate into the endosymbiont to be of use. Somehow this seemingly unpromising scheme not only withstood the hazards of evolution but also proved so successful that all endosymbionts retaining copies of transferred genes eventually disappeared.

Today mitochondria, plastids and peroxisomes acquire proteins from the surrounding cytoplasm with the aid of complex transport structures in their bounding membranes. These structures recognize parts of newly made protein molecules as "address tags" specific to each organelle. The transport apparatus then allows the appropriate molecules to travel through the membrane with the help of energy and of specialized proteins (aptly called chaperones). These systems for bringing externally made proteins into the organelles could conceivably have evolved from similar systems for protein secretion that existed in the original membranes of the endosymbionts. In their new function, however, those systems would have to operate from outside to inside.

The adoption of endosymbionts undoubtedly played a critical role in the birth of eukaryotes. But this was not the key event. More significant (and requiring a much larger number of evolutionary innovations) was the long, mysterious process that made such acquisition possible: the slow conversion, over as long as one billion years or more, of a prokaryotic ancestor into a large phagocytic microbe possessing most attributes of modern eukaryotic cells. Science is beginning to lift the veil that shrouds this momentous transformation, without which much of the living world, including humans, would not exist.

When you think of a prokaryotic cell, you probably imagine a membrane that surrounds a disorganized mix of enzymes, DNA, cytoplasm, and other molecules. Your mental image is probably of something primitive and inefficient. Two researchers from Georg-August Universität in Germany argue in this article that prokaryotes are actually highly efficient and contain "functional compartments." Dr. Michael Hoppert, a research fellow, and Dr. Frank

Mayer, a professor, explain some of their work, which shows that water molecules within the cytoplasm of prokaryotic cells are not all created equal. They hypothesize that water close to the cell membrane is structured and of relatively high density, while the next layer is less tightly packed. The inner core of water molecules may be more like free water in a test tube. The authors suggest that since, experimentally, enzymes prefer less dense water, the layer of less dense water in a prokaryotic cell may actually serve as a unique "functional compartment." Bringing enzymes together in this compartment would be very efficient and organized—not bad for the lowly prokaryote! —JL

"Prokaryotes"
by Michael Hoppert and Frank Mayer
American Scientist, November–December, 1999

What's in a name? A lot, sometimes. A name might betray an underlying assumption—some might even call it a prejudice—as it does in cell biology.

Take, for example, the names assigned to the two major classes of cells. The cells found in plants and animals are called *eukaryotes*, literally, "true nucleus." In contrast, bacterial cells are *prokaryotes*, a designation intended to convey their relatively primitive status as proto-cells and possible forerunners to the eukaryotes.

The basis for this nomenclature lies in the organizational complexity of the eukaryotes on the one hand

and the relative simplicity of the prokaryotes on the other. Such differences became evident early in the 20th century, when improvements in microscopy allowed scientists to get a detailed view inside cells. They noted that both cell types contain a large cellular compartment, known as the *cytoplasm*, which is surrounded by a membrane. But they also noted additional membranous compartments within the eukaryotic cytoplasm that were absent from the prokaryotic cytoplasm. With more sophisticated microscopic techniques, scientists found an additional distinction between the two cell classes. Eukaryotic cells gain structural support from an internal network of fibrous proteins called a *cytoskeleton*, whereas prokaryotes gain their primary structural support from a rigid wall that surrounds the cell. But for purposes of defining the two classes, scientists still focus mainly on the issue of compartments.

One compartment in particular serves as the defining distinction between eukaryotes and prokaryotes. This is the nucleus, the membrane-delineated compartment that houses eukaryotic DNA. There are other organizational distinctions: Prokaryotes do not contain any of the other specialized membrane-bounded compartments found in the typical eukaryote. They do not, for example, contain mitochondria, lysosomes, or peroxisomes.

Throughout this century, cell biologists have refined their understanding of the eukaryotic compartments. Each compartment is a sort of subcellular organ—in fact the compartments are called organelles—housing all of the elements necessary to perform a specific metabolic function. For example, mitochondria generate chemical energy with which to power all the cell's other activities. Lysosomes and peroxisomes contain enzymes that degrade macromolecules. Each organelle operates efficiently because it bundles together all of the biomolecules required to perform a particular task.

In contrast, prokaryotes lack membranous organelles and a typical eukaryotic cytoskeleton. Therefore biomolecules are commonly supposed to be scattered randomly throughout the prokaryotic cytoplasm. From this notion comes another: Prokaryotic metabolism is extremely helter-skelter and inefficient. In truth, this is not the case.

Prokaryotic cells perform their biological functions with stunning efficiency. (Anyone who has ever had a badly infected cut can appreciate just how rapidly bacteria multiply.) So it seems illogical to think of prokaryotes as a bag of randomly distributed chemicals. It makes more sense to suppose that, even without membrane-bounded compartments and a eukaryotic-like cytoskeleton, the molecules required for a particular metabolic activity are grouped together into areas that we like to call functional compartments. The idea of a functional compartment is somewhat analogous to functional areas in a loft apartment. The apartment lacks walls, yet it is possible to identify a "kitchen area" that contains all of the appliances and utensils required to efficiently prepare and eat food. Of course, in the case of the loft, someone has deliberately placed the appliances and utensils in the functional kitchen area. Since the loft does not offer an aqueous environment, these objects are not expected to drift off.

The same cannot be said of the prokaryotic cell. Although cell biologists can discern a sophisticated cellular architecture, cellular components are not deliberately grouped together. Furthermore, the internal environment is aqueous, so compartments could conceivably drift off. Given these factors, how do functional compartments arise and how are they maintained? Studies in our laboratory and others suggest that functional compartments arise spontaneously as a result of the intrinsic properties of the biomolecules themselves and the way they interact with water in the cytoplasm. We have also found that the specific structure of water itself can influence the level of enzyme activity in particular microenvironments.

Prokaryotic Compartments

Until the middle of the 20th century, scientists did not clearly distinguish between prokaryotes and eukaryotes. Based on their observations of these cells under the light microscope, they classified bacteria as very primitive eukaryotic cells. Under the increased magnification of the electron microscope, they first glimpsed the profound organizational differences that now distinguish the two cell types. It was then that the terms "prokaryote" and "eukaryote" came to be widely used by scientists.

More modern electron microscopes have increasingly refined the picture of the prokaryotic cell. They have also made cell biologists aware that some prokaryotes—specifically, a class of bacteria known as

Gram-negative bacteria—are actually encircled by two membranes. Just a few millionths of a meter inside the outer membrane there is the cytoplasmic membrane. Between these two membranes are the *murein sacculus*, a major cell-wall component, and an aqueous compartment called the *periplasmic space*. The periplasmic space is involved in various biochemical pathways, including, for example, the degradation or export of proteins and the extrusion of noxious compounds from the cell.

This refined picture of the prokaryotic cell also extends to structures involved in cell locomotion. Some prokaryotes swim through their environment with the aid of a whiplike appendage called a *flagellum*. Powered by molecular motors, flagella rotate and in this way propel bacteria through their environments. All parts of the flagellum, including its molecular motor, are composed of protein. The motor is anchored in the cytoplasmic membrane and exposed to the cytoplasm. A part of the flagellum that connects the motor with the flagellar filament protrudes across the periplasmic space, the murein sacculus and the outer membrane. The flagellar filament is located in the cell's external environment. Hence the flagellum, an organelle *per se*, spans a number of compartments: the cytoplasm, the cytoplasmic membrane (a functional compartment), the periplasmic space, the outer membrane (again, a functional compartment), and the external environment.

With the exception of the cytoplasm proper and the periplasmic space, no membranous compartments can regularly be found in prokaryotes. But that is not to say that identifiable compartments are entirely lacking, either. Inside the cell, several more distinct compartments can be described. Some of these were evident even in the earliest days of prokaryotic research. Using light microscopes, cell biologists could detect small, highly refractive granules in the cytoplasm of certain prokaryotes. These granules are now known as *inclusion bodies*. They appear to be storage granules, enclosing large aggregates of water-insoluble materials, such as fats and starches. Materials inside the inclusion bodies are degraded into smaller fragments that are released into the cytoplasm when they are required to fuel a metabolic activity.

Scientists now understand something about the biochemistry of inclusion bodies. Among the fats often found inside are long chains of fatty acids called poly-hydroxyalkanoates (PHAs). Like most fats, PHAs repel water, so, naturally, they repel the aqueous cytoplasm.

However, the enzymes that synthesize PHAs are soluble in water, which leads to an interesting situation. While they are being synthesized, PHAs *are* linked to the enzymes and form a complex, part of which is water-soluble and part of which is not. Eventually, the complex organizes itself into a sphere in which the water-soluble enzymes form the shell, shielding the water-insoluble fatty molecules within. Water is expelled from the interior of this sphere, creating a water-free fatty internal compartment separated from the aqueous cytoplasm by a boundary of water-soluble enzymes. Research conducted in the laboratory of

Alexander Steinbüchel, now at the University of Münster in Germany, and his colleagues demonstrated that as the PHA inclusion bodies mature, other water-soluble molecules—including small proteins called phasins—are added to the growing circumference of the boundary layer, while more PHAs are added to the interior compartment.

A big part of the cell's interior space is given over to the bacterial chromosome. This single, very long and circular piece of DNA—on which lie all of the bacterium's essential genes—is found in an area that serves as a nucleus-equivalent. This area is termed the *nucleoid*. (Additional genes are situated on smaller circles or linear strands of DNA, called *plasmids*, found in the cytoplasm.) Although the nucleoid is not delimited by a membrane, it nevertheless exhibits an organizational structure of the highest complexity.

In most bacteria, the chromosome attaches to the cytoplasmic membrane at one point and branches out from there, so that the nucleoid gives the overall impression of being shaped like coral. This shape is maintained by proteins that bind to the DNA, causing certain regions to be highly coiled, whereas others are more loosely wound. Other proteins are also associated with the nucleoid, and these are required to replicate the DNA, regulate gene expression and help apportion DNA into daughter cells during cell division.

The differentially coiled regions give rise to distinct domains within the chromosome. The typical bacterial chromosome has about 100 such domains. It is possible that these domains correspond to groups of genes that all need to be either expressed or repressed at the same time, and so they have important functional significance.

Under the microscope, the cytoplasm of bacteria appears uniform, save for the occasional inclusion body. No structure is visible that corrals biomolecules into a particular spot. And yet few metabolic enzymes in the prokaryote are found to be alone. Instead, enzymes that act together in a sequence of metabolic events tend to join together into larger functional units. Victor Norris at the University of Rouen in France coined the term "enzoskeleton" to describe such enzyme assemblages. There exists evidence to suggest that enzymes may well be arrayed within these complexes in the same sequence in which they perform their functions. This would lead to a high metabolic efficiency, as the product of one enzymatic reaction would immediately serve as the substrate for the next, with very little loss of product between steps.

One well-documented example is the multiprotein complex called the *cellulosome* found on the surface of the bacterium *Clostridium thermocellum*. This complex allows the bacterium to adhere to and degrade cellulose, the main polymer found in the cell walls and woody stalks of plants. Under conditions where oxygen is scarce, as it is in lake sediments, bacteria such as *Clostridium* can obtain energy by degrading cellulose and other biological polymers from decayed plants. The cellulosome includes over 14 degradative enzymes called *cellulases* bound together onto a proteinaceous scaffold (known variously as scaffoldin or CipA), which is anchored to the bacterial cell surface.

The nucleoid, the flagellum, and the cellulosome provide examples of associations of many different protein species, some of which are structural and some of which are catalytic. Several other protein aggregates that are built up of large numbers of similar units can be found within the cytoplasm. One of these is the proteasome. This barrel-shaped structure is composed of digestive enzymes, which degrade proteins into their constituent parts. Another barrel-shaped structure called a chaperonin contains repeats of an enzyme whose function is to fold freshly synthesized proteins into their mature conformation.

Responses to Water

The notion that enzymes could be grouped into defined functional compartments has inspired us to explore other types of organization. In particular, we are interested in learning how the microenvironments of the aqueous cytoplasm affect enzyme organization. We have been particularly interested in the interaction between enzymes and the water in the cytoplasm, since we believe this interaction to be of the utmost importance in defining another type of functional compartment.

We have come to our proposition by considering how closely enzymatic studies conducted *in vitro* approximate the actual interactions that may be important *in vivo*. Some people will correctly point out that several complex metabolic systems can function, disaggregated, *in vitro*. But we do not believe that this is an accurate simulation of what actually takes place in living cells. *In vitro*, the enzymes making up the system are the only ones in the test tube, so they are free from confounding interactions with other components. But this is not realistic. In the living cell, enzymatic systems have to work in a cytoplasm replete with proteins and other compounds. We strongly believe that in this situation, defined enzymatic activities are only possible when the enzymes are maintained at defined distances from other macromolecules. And that is only possible in a structured cytoplasm. Our studies suggest that water itself is an important part of this structure. In 1984, James Clegg at the Scripps Institution of Oceanography in La Jolla, California wrote, "in virtually all interactions, the participating macromolecules first 'see' each other through their water structures."

In other words, the behavior of enzymes—the speed and efficiency with which they carry out their functions and the nature of their interactions—is influenced by the aqueous environment in which they function. This at first may seem a trivial statement, because all agents that are dissolved or suspended in water can modify enzyme activities. Salts, amino acids, proteins, and organic solvents can alter the stability and activity of enzymes. What is less evident is that dissolved components may influence enzymes indirectly by altering the actual structure of the water surrounding the enzymes.

Reversed Micelles

To study further the interactions between water and enzyme activities, we have developed a versatile model system for structured cytoplasm. Water can exist in various states. It can be a solid or a liquid, for example. But even liquid water can take on various forms. This becomes particularly evident inside the artificial system of a *reversed micelle*. A conventional micelle is formed when water surrounds a sphere of *amphiphilic* molecules. These are molecules in which one end is water soluble, while the other is water insoluble. To form a micelle, water-soluble heads of amphiphilic molecules maintain contact with the water, while the water-insoluble tails are tucked inside. A reversed micelle is just the opposite. The water is held inside a sphere of amphiphilic molecules. A model of cellular water structure developed by Philippa Wiggins at the University of Auckland in New Zealand helped us to understand the role of water in reversed micelles.

Depending on the size of the reversed micelle and the location of the water molecules within it, the water exhibits at least two structures. Water that is close to the periphery of the micelle, in direct contact with the barrier molecules (called surfactants), differs from water nearer the center of the reversed micelle. And both of these structures differ from free, chemically pure water.

The water molecules closest to the surfactants in the boundary layer are less free to move about and are more densely packed than are the molecules in free water. Densely packed water molecules are less likely to form hydrogen bonds with neighboring water molecules than are the molecules in free water.

In contrast, water farther away from the surfactant boundary is less densely packed than is free water. The low-density water balances out the effects of the high-density water and brings the entire system into thermodynamic equilibrium. Low-density water forms a greater number of hydrogen bonds than does pure water. The highly bonded low-density water results in a regular network of water molecules, resembling somewhat the molecular lattice of ice. In addition to maintaining a regular structure, low-density water is less electrically charged, less reactive, and more viscous than regular water.

In living cells, all cellular compartments and macromolecular assemblies affect water structure and create a framework of low- and high-density water. This in turn introduces some heterogeneity into the cytoplasm. Thus water structures are important parts of cellular compartmentalization. The water structure in an area of the cytoplasm determines the physical properties of a compartment and in this way influences the activity of enzymes in that area.

It is possible to measure the vibrational frequency of proteins dissolved in low-density water, using the reversed-micelle system. In this system proteins surrounded by low-density water do indeed experience a decrease in vibrational frequency compared with proteins dissolved in free water. The vibrational frequency influences the activity of the enzymatic reaction. For example, lowering the vibrational frequency of an enzyme may shift upwards the temperature at which the enzyme achieves its optimal rate of reaction.

The reversed micelle system has allowed us to get at some additional facets of the relation between enzyme activity and water structure. Our experimental setup is quite simple. The reversed micelle will form spontaneously when we supply the proper, experimentally determined, proportions of water, surfactant, and solvent. We can alter the size of the reversed micelle by varying the water concentration, and we can add enzymes and other water-soluble compounds to the internal aqueous compartment, until we achieve the conditions we are trying to study.

In our studies, we have varied the size of the reversed micelles and have discovered that all of the enzymes we tested achieve their optimal efficiency when the reversed micelle reaches a particular size. Interestingly enough, that size roughly corresponds to the dimensions of the water-filled spaces, such as the periplasm, found in the average prokaryote. Furthermore, physicochemical properties of the surface provided by the surfactant structures resemble the surface properties of macromolecules in the living cell. So it seems reasonable to us that water within these structures assumes an array similar to that seen in reversed micelles. Given that we feel comfortable that reversed micelles mimic the actual conditions inside the prokaryotic cell, we conclude that most enzymes have evolved to operate best within a particular water structure.

At the moment, we are considering ways to expand our studies of water structure into the living cell. Were such experiments possible, we would not be surprised to discover that enzymes are positioned inside the prokaryotes so that their active sites sit within an area whose water structure promotes optimal activity. The level of enzymatic activities we measure inside the reverse micelles may well reflect the real level of activity inside the living cell. These activity levels cannot be observed under conditions that promote the inappropriate water structures.

We therefore believe that when considering prokaryote organization, it is important to think about possible microenvironments within the cytoplasm, one form of which may be brought about by differential structures of water. We propose that a boundary of structured water approximately 2 to 10 nanometers thick (one nanometer is one-billionth of a meter) can be found abutting a cell membrane and other macromolecular cell structures.

Within this boundary, we would expect high-density water to lie closest to the cell membrane, followed by a layer of low-density water. Further inside the cell, but only at some distance from other macromolecular surfaces, we would expect to find a region of free water. Furthermore, we would expect enzymes to be preferentially positioned in layers of structured water. In our experiments, enzymes seem to function best in low-density water, and this is where we would predict finding enzymes in living cells. Therefore, we predict that the layers of structured water are likewise a functional compartment, such as inclusion bodies, the nucleoid, and other specialized macromolecular structures.

Reprinted with permission from *American Scientist*.

With all the careful distinctions that biologists have made between prokaryotes and eukaryotes, it would be easy to ignore any evidence that does not fit within the current model. Eukaryotes have a nucleus; prokaryotes do not. Eukaryotes have membrane-bound organelles; prokaryotes do not. Or do they? It took a veterinarian to shake up the whole world of biology by insisting that prokaryotes do indeed have membrane-bound organelles. Dr. Roberto Docampo, a professor of veterinary pathobiology at the University of Illinois at Urbana-Champaign, examined some black specks in the cytoplasm of the prokaryote Agrobacterium tumefaciens *and was surprised to find tiny organelles similar to acido-calcisomes in eukaryotes. Acidocalcisomes store acidic calcium within the cell. That they were found in bacteria serves as a good reminder not to take any definition in biology as the final word and to always keep a questioning, scientific frame of mind.* —JL

"Veterinarian Finds Evolutionary Link Between Humans and Bacteria"
by Michael Abrams
Discover, January 2004

We higher forms of life have always distinguished our-selves from our single-celled microscopic friends. After all, we have a brain and a more interesting sex life. And we have organelles, tiny structures that are the basic workhorses inside complex cells. Organelles have their own membranes and perform such functions as producing energy or gobbling up foreign invaders. Such luxuries don't normally go to a single cell.

Or so we thought. This year Roberto Docampo, a professor of veterinary pathobiology at the University of Illinois at Urbana-Champaign, found that the bacterium *Agrobacterium tumefaciens*, which causes crown gall disease in plants, does indeed have organelles. His discovery muddies the distinction between eukaryotes (organisms with nuclei in their cells) and prokaryotes (single-celled life-forms without nuclei). It also sheds light on how eukaryotes and prokaryotes evolved.

Docampo was hardly the first to notice that prokaryotes have mysterious black specks floating in their cytoplasm. Yet he is one of the few ever to study them. When he focused an electron microscope on the specks, he discovered that they were actually pouchlike compartments with membranes. He then discovered that they contained pyrophosphatase, an enzyme that can shuttle proteins in and out of a structure to maintain its acidity. On further examination, it turned out that the black specks are a type of organelle—called an acidocalcisome—that is also found in certain single-celled eukaryotes.

Although the precise function of acidocalcisomes is not understood, Docampo says their discovery implies that organelles may have been in cells before our evolutionary ancestors and those of today's bacteria diverged. "They are really the same organelle that probably originated in bacteria and was conserved during evolution," he says. "Bacteria are more similar to eukaryotes than we thought."

Reprinted with permission from *Discover Magazine*.

You have learned that mitochondria and plastids may have arisen through the capture of one cell by another, leading to a symbiotic relationship between both and the rise of the eukaryotic cell. The general theory is well accepted, but researchers are still deciphering the fine details. One key area of research is genome reduction. That is, the mitochondria and plastids of today have a few genes that are separate from the cell in which they reside. This small number of genes is not enough for the mitochondria or plastids to live separately. At one point in history, however, the ancestors of mitochondria and plastids did have enough genes to live alone. Gene transfer is the process in which most of the ancestor cell's genes moved into the nucleus of the host cell once they were living symbiotically together. In this article, Sabrina D. Dyall, Mark T. Brown, and Patricia J. Johnson from the Department of Microbiology, Immunology, and Molecular Genetics at the University of California, Los Angeles, review the most recent advances in our understanding of how the ancestors of mitochondria and plastids changed from cells living alone into the subcellular organelles of today. —JL

"Ancient Invasions: From Endosymbionts to Organelles"
by Sabrina D. Dyall, Mark T. Brown,
and Patricia J. Johnson
Science, April 9, 2004

The acquisitions of mitochondria and plastids were important events in the evolution of the eukaryotic cell, supplying it with compartmentalized bioenergetic and biosynthetic factories. Ancient invasions by eubacteria through symbiosis more than a billion years ago initiated these processes. Advances in geochemistry, molecular phylogeny, and cell biology have offered insight into complex molecular events that drove the evolution of endosymbionts into contemporary organelles. In losing their autonomy, endosymbionts lost the bulk of their genomes, necessitating the evolution of elaborate mechanisms for organelle biogenesis and metabolite exchange. In the process, symbionts acquired many host-derived properties, lost much of their eubacterial identity, and were transformed into extraordinarily diverse organelles that reveal complex histories that we are only beginning to decipher.

Analyses of mitochondrial genes and their genomic organization and distribution indicate that mitochondrial genomes are derived from an α-proteobacterium–like ancestor, probably due to a single ancient invasion of an Archea-type host that occurred >1.5 billion years ago (Ga).[1] Whether the host cell was already eukaryotic is unclear although all contemporary eukaryotes examined contain some genes contributed by this symbiont.[2]

How the proto-mitochondrial ancestor invaded and avoided elimination by the host has generated many hypotheses since the symbiosis theory was revived by Margulis.[3] Some account for the concurrent origin of eukaryotes and mitochondria.[4, 5] These hypotheses propose a metabolically driven symbiosis where the host is a methanogenic archaean that associated with a methanotrophic proteobacterium to obtain essential compounds, e.g., hydrogen.[4] The hydrogen hypothesis accounts for both mitochondrial aerobic pathways and anaerobic pathways in organelles of possible mitochondrial ancestry, e.g., hydrogenosomes.[4] Notably, these scenarios posit the invasion to have occurred under anoxic conditions because both host and symbiont were capable of anaerobic metabolism. In contrast, an "aerobic" origin theory hypothesizes that the symbiosis was driven by an aerobic proteobacterium relieving an anaerobic host from oxygen tension.[6]

Fossils of red algae-like organisms confirm that multicellular plastid-bearing eukaryotes existed 1.2 Ga, and there is evidence of eukaryotic algaelike organisms around 1.5 Ga. Mitochondria appear to predate the advent of plastids; therefore, the proto mitochondrial invasion is believed to have occurred >1.5 Ga.[7] Oxygenic photosynthesis is thought to have started 3.5 Ga, with oxygen levels becoming substantial by about 2.2 Ga, as intimated by the discovery of oxidized rocks.[8] The sharp rise in oxygen 2.2 Ga supports the aerobically driven origin for mitochondrial endosymbiosis.[6] However, carbon isotope signatures indicate that archaea and proteobacteria coexisted around 2.7 Ga, giving support to the anaerobic-driven hypotheses.[4, 5] Thus, it is not clear what evolutionary bottleneck forged the irreversible union of the endosymbiont and its host.

Of Mitochondria and Hydrogenosomes

Several microaerophilic protists, e.g., trichomonads, anaerobic fungi, and ciliates, do not have mitochondria but possess doublemembraned organelles called hydrogenosomes, which produce adenosine triphosphate (ATP) fermentatively. Unlike mitochondria, which use pyruvate dehydrogenase for pyruvate oxidation, *Trichomonas* hydrogenosomes decarboxylate pyruvate with pyruvate:ferredoxin oxidoreductase (PFOR), which transfers electrons to an [Fe]-hydrogenase, ultimately producing ATP, H_2, and CO_2.[9] PFOR and hydrogenase are typically found in anaerobic bacteria, and the origin of the eukaryotic homologs is unknown, although it appears that eukaryotic PFOR has a single origin.[2] However, phylogenetic analyses of a few protein-coding genes have suggested a common ancestry for hydrogenosomes and mitochondria, as do similarities in organelle biogenesis.[10]

Hydrogenosomes appear to lack a genome,[10] and ultimately defining the protomitochondrion/hydrogenosome relationship will be circumstantial, because this must be proteome-based. For instance, phylogenetic analyses of >400 nucleus-encoded yeast mitochondrial proteins have revealed that 50% are of eukaryotic origin and 50% of prokaryotic origin. Of the latter, only 20% are α-proteobacteria-derived.[6] In a reverse approach, where α-proteobacterial genomes were compared with eukaryotic genomes, it was found that only 14 to 16% of mitochondrial proteins were of α-proteobacterial origin,[11] implying that most of the mitochondrial proteome is of nonendosymbiotic origin. Thus, the discovery of a few proteins of mitochondrial endosymbiont descent in *Trichomonas* hydrogenosomes,[2, 10] which also bear atypical anaerobic metabolic enzymes,[9] does not constitute definitive evidence that the hydrogenosome arose linearly from the proto-mitochondrion. The available data are too limited to distinguish between scenarios A and B for the origin of the trichomonad hydrogenosome. The most parsimonious scenario A is that hydrogenosomes are vertically derived from the proto-mitochondrion and acquired "unconventional" proteins by horizontal gene transfer. Scenario B posits that after gene transfer, the generation of several eukaryotic-specific proteins, and a primordial protein translocation machinery, the proto-mitochondrion was lost in some cells. A second invasion by an anaerobic eubacterium subsequently occurred, giving rise to a proto-hydrogenosome that acquired proteins generated by the prior endosymbiotic event. Such protein recruitment has been noted in chloroplasts for some Calvin cycle proteins that have a proteobacterial origin.[12] Clearly, further appraisal of the hydrogenosomal proteome, particularly of eukaryotic-type proteins, is required before conclusively assigning an origin for this organelle. The origin of proposed mitochondrial remnants[13] found in three independent lineages—*Entamoeba* (mitosome), *Giardia* (mitosome), and a microsporidian (mitochondrial relic)—should likewise be viewed tentatively. These structures have been defined by the presence of a single mitochondrial-like protein, which is different in each case (either cpn60, Hsp70, or IscS). Whether these structures are ultimately found to be directly derived from mitochondria will await proteomic analyses.

Invasion of the "Little Green Slaves"

Historically, the endosymbiotic theory of chloroplast evolution can be traced back to Mereschkowsky's hypothesis in 1905 that plastids are reduced forms of cyanobacteria acting as "little workers, green slaves" within the cell.[14] Phylogenetic, structural, and biochemical analyses have now confirmed that a single symbiotic association between a cyanobacterium and a mitochondriate eukaryote between 1.2 and 1.5 Ga led to the birth of primary plastids of algae, plants, and glaucophytes.[7, 15] The type of cyanobacteria that gave rise to plastids is still being investigated. Remarkably, plastids have spread by secondary endosymbiosis, whereby photosynthetic eukaryotes were engulfed by nonphotosynthetic eukaryotes. The resulting secondary plastids underwent genome reduction and in some cases even lost their photosynthetic functions, e.g., apicoplasts.[15]

From Invaders to Captives: Genome Reduction

A critical step in the transition from autonomous endosymbiont to organelle was genome reduction. Contemporary mitochondrial genomes range from 3 to 67 protein-coding genes,[1] and chloroplast genomes from 50 to 200.[16] Many endosymbiont genes have been lost,[11] and most of the retained ones were transferred to the nucleus. Productive gene transfer would require serendipitous landing near active promoters or reacquiring promoters used by the host. Thus, genes would exist in duplicate until the system evolved a targeting machinery to relocate the gene product to the proto-organelle.

A reduced, common subset of retained genes points toward a rapid ancient transfer and loss of the mitochondrial endosymbiont genome.[1] Genetic transfer from endosymbiont genomes to the nucleus is, however, not limited to ancient events: Recent, frequent, and functional transfers have been demonstrated for mitochondrial[17] and chloroplast[18] genes within angiosperms. Although transfers seem to have reached a plateau in most eukaryotic groups,[1, 17, 19] a selectable marker gene has been shown to move from the mitochondrial to the nuclear genome of transformed yeast at a surprisingly high frequency.[20] Likewise, chloroplast to nucleus gene transfer has been observed at comparatively high frequencies.[21, 22] In this case, an intron within the marker gene was recovered following transfer, arguing against a cDNA-mediated mechanism.[21] Large segments of mitochondrial and/or chloroplast ancestral genomes found in several nuclei similarly support DNA transfer en bloc.[23] On the other hand, the presence of nuclear genes that appear to be derived from edited mitochondrial transcripts[24] indicates that both RNA- and DNA-mediated mechanisms drive genome transfer and reduction.

Why have organellar genomes retained a few genes, thus necessitating the retention of an entire machinery for genome replication, RNA expression, and translation? Analyses of 750 yeast mitochondrial proteins indicate that $\sim 25\%$ are involved in the maintenance of a genome encoding only eight highly hydrophobic membrane proteins[25] believed to be retained to avoid mistargeting. One of these, cytochrome c oxidase subunit 2 (Cox2), which is mitochondrion-encoded in most eukaryotes, is found in both nuclear and mitochondrial genomes of certain legumes, indicating a recent gene transfer. The nucleus-encoded Cox2 displays decreased local hydrophobicity relative to mitochondrial Cox2, a change demonstrated to be necessary for its import into mitochondria.[26]

Organelle Biogenesis

Endosymbiotic organelle biogenesis involves two critical events: division and preprotein translocation. Both processes are driven by a combination of symbiont- and host-derived proteins. Two proteins, FtsZ and the dynamin-related protein (Drp1), play key roles in mitochondrial and plastid division. FtsZ, of endosymbiont origin, is a protein essential for eubacterial division and is found in most chloroplasts, but appears to be limited to the mitochondria of certain single-celled eukaryotes.[27] Drp1, necessary for outer mitochondrial membrane fission, is closely related to dynamin, a eukaryotic-specific protein required to sever membranes during endocytosis.[28] Importing proteins encoded by nuclear genes was a second prerequisite for organelle biogenesis. Extensive studies of mitochondrial[29] and plastidal[30, 31] protein translocation machineries have revealed several common features.

Mitochondrial proteins have four destinations: the outer membrane (OM), the intermembrane space (IMS), the inner membrane (IM), or the matrix. Most proteins, including outer membrane proteins, are translocated by the TOM (translocase of the outer mitochondrial membrane) complex and then directed toward the inner membrane TIM23 (translocase of the inner mitochondrial membrane) translocon for insertion, or translocation into the IMS or the matrix. A number of inner membrane–spanning, eukaryotic-specific proteins with internal targeting signals, including the adenosine diphosphate (ADP)/ATP carrier (AAC) and some Tim proteins, are diverted toward the TIM22 translocon for insertion.[29]

Within chloroplasts, proteins can be targeted to six compartments: the outer envelope (OE), the inner envelope (IE), the intermembrane space, the stroma, the thylakoid membrane, or the lumen. Translocation through the outer envelope occurs via the TOC (translocase of the outer chloroplast envelope) complex, and the inner envelope via the TIC (translocase of the inner chloroplast envelope) complex.[30] Thylakoid targeting occurs through four mechanisms.[31]

The Origin of Targeting Peptides

Most nuclear-encoded mitochondrial, hydrogenosomal, and plastidal precursors have an N-terminal presequence that is necessary at multiple translocation steps.[10, 29–32] Thus, the presequence in these systems would have coevolved with the translocon. How did these presequences get appended to hundreds of genes? In plant mitochondria and chloroplasts, some presequences are partitioned on several exons, suggesting exon shuffling and alternative splicing to be mechanisms for presequence evolution.[33] Alternatively, N-terminal presequences could have been created de novo by promoter-region duplication and mutation. Some recently transferred mitochondrial genes have been observed to scavenge mitochondrial pre-sequence units from previously transferred genes encoding mitochondrial proteins.[17]

Mitochondrial and plastidal presequences are loosely conserved and enriched in specific amino acid types.[29, 32] In contrast, hydrogenosomal targeting prese-quences, although shorter, show stronger primary sequence conservation.[10] In secondary plastids, e.g., the apicoplast, the existence of two extra membranes neces-sitated the creation of a bipartite presequence, consisting of a signal peptide for entrance into the secretory path-way fused to a "traditional" plastid transit peptide for crossing the two inner plastid envelopes.[33]

An important factor during the evolution of the proto-plastid was the presence of the mitochondrion. Coordinated evolution of both the mitochondrial and proto-plastid protein import machineries would be required for apparently conflicting reasons: to avoid mistargeting of potentially harmful proteins or to promote dual targeting of proteins shared by both organelles. Chloroplast and plant mitochondrial presequences share similarities,[32] yet specifically target proteins to their respective organelles. Interestingly, chloroplast transit peptides can target proteins to nonplant mitochondria,[34] raising the possibility that the plastid transit peptide evolved from the mitochondrial presequence. Addi-tionally, plant mitochondrial Tom receptors for presequence-bearing precursors differ markedly from their nonplant counterparts,[35] presumably to prevent mis-targeting. Nevertheless, dual-targeted proteins have been identified that use either tandem or ambiguous prese-quences. Such mechanisms would eliminate the need for several gene copies for shared biochemical functions.

The transit peptide may have allowed the delivery of novel functions into the evolving organelle. DNA encoding this peptide could land at the 5′ end of nonendo-symbiotic-derived genes and would be retained if the encoded proteins conferred an advantage. Over millions of years, new pathways would evolve and "missing" elements, e.g., the enzymes in the mitochondrial Krebs cycle that are of nonproteobacterial origin,[36] could have been replaced in old pathways.

Mitochondria have ribosome-binding sites to which some mRNAs have been localized. The majority of mitochondrion-bound messages are of prokaryotic origin, whereas mRNAs of eukaryotic origin are pref-erentially translated on cytosolic ribosomes.[37] The preferential targeting of the prokaryotic-type mRNAs to mitochondria may reflect an early targeting mechanism prior to the advent of protein targeting signals.

Building the Protein Import Machine

Mitochondrial and plastid protein translocases have a dual origin. The emerging picture is that many translo-cases of the OM are of eukaryotic origin, those in the IM are of mixed origin, and soluble chaperones primarily bear prokaryotic traits. Mitochondrial Tom40, which forms the channel of the OM protein import pore, has strong secondary structure similarity to eubacterial OM beta-barrel porins but no notable primary sequence sim-ilarity.[38] Two beta-barrel proteins, a porin from *Neisseri*[39] and a *Trichomonas* hydrogenosomal membrane protein, Hmp35,[40] can be targeted and inserted into mitochondrial membranes despite a lack of sequence similarity to any mitochondrial proteins. Furthermore, both proteins assemble into oligomers of similar size to those formed in their respective homologous systems.[39, 40] Thus, it appears that the targeting of beta-barrel proteins in the mitochondrial OM has an ancient origin and that beta-barrel proteins such as Tom40 and the mitochondrial-type porin may have arisen de novo by convergent evolution into pore-type proteins. A newly characterized mitochondrial OM protein, Sam50, is essential for the assembly of Tom40 and porin.[41-43] Sam50 has a putative beta-barrel domain and is a member of the Omp85 family of proteins, which in *Neisseria* have been invoked in eubacterial outer envelope biogenesis.[44, 45] Phylogenetic analyses indicate a common ancestry for proteobacterial and mitochondrial members of the Omp85 family.[43] It is possible that Sam50 was a primordial translocase that assisted the assembly of beta-barrel pores as they were being invented or recruited. In contrast to the eukaryotic-specific Tom40 protein, the chloroplast OE protein that forms the hydrophilic pore,[30] Toc75, is of eubacterial origin. Its homolog in the cyanobacterium *Synechocystis*, upon reconstitution in artificial bilayers, formed a voltage-gated peptide-sensitive channel.[46] Interestingly, plastidal Toc75, like mitochondrial Sam50, forms part of the Omp85 family,[43] thus showing that Omp85-like proteins were recruited for the biogenesis of two independent organelles, suggesting that their acquisition was critical.

The mitochondrial IM proteins Tim17, Tim22, and Tim23 are divergent homologs with domains distantly related to the bacterial LivH permease involved in translocating branched amino acids.[47] A similar relationship has been shown between chloroplast Tic20 and LivH.[46] The homology between Tim23 and Tim22, two channel proteins that specifically translocate either presequence-bearing precursors or eukaryotic-specific membrane proteins, suggests the existence of a primordial channel that eventually duplicated after the advent of transit peptides and the invention of inner membrane proteins. Hmp31, a *Trichomonas* hydrogenosomal membrane protein related to mitochondrial AAC, can be imported into yeast mitochondria using the specific TIM22 pathway for AAC.[48] Surprisingly, a basic local alignment search tool (BLAST)[49] search of the *Trichomonas vaginalis* genome[50, 51] did not reveal homologs to any yeast translocases involved in this pathway. Although it cannot be excluded that these genes are yet to be sequenced, it appears that despite our predictions,[10, 40, 48] the hydrogenosomal and mitochondrial translocons are divergent or may have different origins.

Mitochondrial Oxa1 is involved in the post- or cotranslational insertion of certain inner membrane proteins of prokaryotic origin.[52] Oxa1 has both a bacterial homolog, YidC, that is involved in Sec-independent membrane protein insertion and a thylakoidal homolog, Alb3, that functionally complements bacterial YidC.[52] Thus, this family of membrane protein translocase is functionally conserved in bacteria, mitochondria, and plastids.

Within plastids, two membrane protein translocons of endosymbiotic origin coexist in thylakoids: a post-translational SRP (signal-recognition particle)– dependent pathway for polytopic membrane proteins and a Tat (twin-arginine translocase) pathway for insertion of folded proteins. A third Sec-dependent pathway of endosymbiotic origin and a fourth "spontaneous" pathway of possible eukaryotic origin that transports substrates of cyanobacterial origin[31] are also present.

Conclusion

Ancient eubacterial invasions gave rise to mitochondria and plastids and had an enormous impact on eukary-ogenesis and the metabolism and homeostasis of eukaryotes. Although genomic analyses indicate that specific endosymbionts gave birth to these organelles, proteomics reveal a surprisingly large contribution from the host, multiple symbioses, and/or horizontal gene transfers. These studies attest to the flexibility of the eukaryotic cell while simultaneously revealing the conservation of mechanisms underlying the evolution of plastids, mitochondria, and derived organelles. Common mechanisms for protein translocation exist, yet specific targeting signals, translocation mechanisms, and retention of organellar-specific proteins have permitted the cohabitation of mitochondria and plastids. Despite considerable advances in our understanding of organelle evolution and biogenesis, future genomic and proteomic analyses promise to accelerate our understanding of these vital features of eukaryotic cells.

References and Notes

1. M. W. Gray, G. Burger, B. F. Lang, *Science* **283**, 1476 (1999).
2. T. M. Embley, M. van der Giezen, D. S. Horner, P. L. Dyal, P. Foster, *Philos. Trans. R. Soc. Lond. B Biol. Sci.* **358**, 191 (2003).
3. W. Martin, M. Hoffmeister, C. Rotte, K. Henze, *Biol. Chem.* **382**, 1521 (2001).
4. W. Martin, M. Müller, *Nature* **392**, 37 (1998).
5. D. Moreira, P. Lopez-Garcia, *J. Mol. Evol.* **47**, 517 (1998).
6. S. G. Andersson, O. Karlberg, B. Canback, C. G. Kurland, *Philos. Trans. R. Soc. Lond. B Biol. Sci.* **358**, 165 (2003).
7. W .Martin, M. J. Russell, *Philos. Trans. R. Soc. Lond. B Biol. Sci.* **358**, 59 (2003).
8. E. G. Nisbet, N. H. Sleep, *Nature* **409**, 1083 (2001).
9. M. Muller, in *Evolutionary Relationships Among Protozoa* G. H. Coombs, M. A.Vickerman, M. A. Sleigh, A. Warren, Eds. (Kluwer, Dordrecht, Netherlands, 1998), pp. 109–131.
10. S. D. Dyall, P. J. Johnson, *Curr. Opin. Microbiol.* **3**, 404 (2000).
11. T. Gabaldon, M. A. Huynen, *Science* **301**, 609 (2003).
12. W. Martin, C. Schnarrenberger, *Curr. Genet.* **32**, 1 (1997).
13. K. Henze, W. Martin, *Nature* **426**, 127 (2003).
14. W. Martin, K. V. Kowallik, *Eur. J. Phycol.* **34**, 287 (1999).
15. J. D. Palmer, *J. Phycol.* **39**, 4 (2003).
16. G. Glockner, A. Rosenthal, K. Valentin, *J. Mol. Evol.* **51**, 382 (2000).
17. K. L. Adams, J. D. Palmer, *Mol. Phylogenet. Evol.* **29**, 380 (2003).
18. R. S. Millen *et al.*, *Plant Cell* **13**, 645 (2001).
19. J. L. Boore, *Nucleic Acids Res.* **27**, 1767 (1999).
20. P. E. Thorsness, T. D. Fox, *Nature* **346**, 376 (1990).
21. C. Y. Huang, M. A. Ayliffe, J. N. Timmis, *Nature* **422**, 72 (2003).
22. S. Stegemann, S. Hartmann, S. Ruf, R. Bock, *Proc. Natl. Acad. Sci. U.S.A.* **100**, 8828 (2003).
23. W. Martin, *Proc. Natl. Acad. Sci. U.S.A.* **100**, 8612 (2003).
24. J. M. Nugent, J. D. Palmer, *Cell* **66**, 473 (1991).
25. A. Sickmann *et al.*, *Proc. Natl. Acad. Sci. U.S.A.* **100**, 13207 (2003).
26. D. O. Daley, R. Clifton, J.Whelan, *Proc. Natl. Acad. Sci. U.S.A.* 99,10510 (2002).
27. K. W. Osteryoung, J. Nunnari, *Science* **302**, 1698 (2003).
28. L. Griparic, A. M. van der Bliek, *Traffic* **2**, 235 (2001).
29. K. N. Truscott, K. Brandner, N. Pfanner, *Curr. Biol.* **13**, R326 (2003).
30. Soll, *Curr. Opin. Plant Biol.* **5**, 529 (2002).
31. C. Robinson, S. J. Thompson, C. Woolhead, *Traffic* **2**, 245 (2001).
32. X. P. Zhang, E. Glaser, *Trends Plant Sci.* **7**, 14 (2002).
33. G. I. McFadden, *Curr. Opin. Plant Biol.* **2,** 513 (1999).

34. N. Peeters, I. Small, *Biochim. Biophys. Acta* **1541**, 54 (2001).

35. D. Macasev, E. Newbigin, J. Whelan, T. Lithgow, *Plant Physiol.* **123**, 811 (2000).

36. C. Schnarrenberger, W. Martin, *Eur. J. Biochem.* **269**, 868 (2002).

37. P. Marc *et al.*, *EMBO Rep.* **3**, 159 (2002).

38. K. Gabriel, S. K. Buchanan, T. Lithgow, *Trends Biochem. Sci.* **26**, 36 (2001).

39. A. Muller *et al.*, *EMBO J.* **21**, 1916 (2002).

40. S. D. Dyall *et al.*, *J. Biol. Chem.* **278**, 30548 (2003).

41. V. Kozjak *et al.*, *J. Biol. Chem.* **278**, 48520 (2003).

42. S. A. Paschen *et al.*, *Nature* **426**, 862 (2003).

43. I. Gentle, K. Gabriel, P. Beech, R. Waller, T. Lithgow, *J. Cell Biol.* **164**, 19 (2004).

44. R. Voulhoux, M. P. Bos, J. Geurtsen, M. Mols, J. Tommassen, *Science* **299**, 262 (2003).

45. S. Genevrois, L. Steeghs, P. Roholl, J. J. Letesson, P. van der Ley, *EMBO J.* **22**, 1780 (2003).

46. S. Reumann, K. Keegstra, *Trends Plant Sci.* **4**, 302 (1999).

47. J. Rassow, P. J. Dekker, S. van Wilpe, M. Meijer, J. Soll, *J. Mol. Biol.* **286**, 105 (1999).

48. S. D. Dyall *et al.*, *Mol. Cell. Biol.* **20**, 2488 (2000).

49. S. F. Altschul, W. Gish, W. Miller, E. W. Myers, D. J. Lipman, *J. Mol. Biol.* **215**, 403 (1990).

50. S. D. Dyall, M. T. Brown, P. J. Johnson, unpublished data.

51. Preliminary *Trichomonas vaginalis* sequence data were obtained from The Institute for Genomic Research through the Web site at www.tigr.org.

52. A. Kuhn, R. Stuart, R. Henry, R. E. Dalbey, *Trends Cell Biol.* **13**, 510 (2003).

53. K. N. Truscott et al., *J. Cell Biol.* **163** ,707 (2003).

The human immune system is a complex and effective defense against invading pathogens. To outsmart the immune cells, invaders have developed some intricate tricks to enter human cells, to grow inside them, and to leave when they have sufficiently multiplied. In this article, Dr. Erich Gulbins, an associate professor at St. Jude Children's Research Hospital in Memphis, Tennessee, and Dr. Florian Lang, a professor at the University of Tübingen in Germany, explain these "tricks." One common tactic for entering a cell is to force it to take up the pathogen by endocytosis, usually by binding to a protein on the cell surface. Some bacteria allow themselves to be phagocytosed by macrophages and then prevent the normal digestion process once inside. In order to meet their growing needs, pathogens that furiously replicate while hidden inside cells can alter the transport proteins in the cell membrane to shuttle in large amounts of glucose, amino acids, and vitamins. When it is finally time to leave, pathogens sometimes simply burst open the cell, but the more sophisticated ones cause cell death. This is desirable because the fragments left after the self-destruction are usually quickly taken up by other cells, and the cycle can begin anew. —JL

"Pathogens, Host-Cell Invasion and Disease"
by Erich Gulbins and Florian Lang
American Scientist, **September–October 2001**

Since the dawn of civilization, infectious diseases have shaped human history. In the Middle Ages, Europe lost up to a third of its population to plague outbreaks. The Spanish flu outbreak during the winter of 1918–19 killed more people—between 25 and 40 million—than did World War I. It was not until 1941, with the development of penicillin, that science could offer a potent weapon against infection, at least against bacterial diseases. But modern medicine is far from having won the war against pathogens, organisms that cause disease. Infectious diseases, including AIDS and malaria, are a severe health problem in the Third World. And in the developed world, bacteria are becoming increasingly resistant to the antibiotic drugs available to combat them.

To develop new treatments against infectious diseases, whether caused by viruses, bacteria, or higher microorganisms, it is important to better understand the nature of infection—the mechanisms and strategies that pathogens use to invade the body's cells as well as overcome the body's defenses against them. New approaches are needed that do not trigger evolutionary countermoves by the pathogens. Such strategies, we hope, might arise from a better understanding of the ways pathogens invade host cells and evade the immune system—an area of research neglected while antibiotics provided easy answers, but clearly essential to providing new weapons for the continuing battle against infectious disease. Recent research has therefore been concentrating on the mechanisms that infectious agents use to gain entrance to their target cells as well as the strategies that the host evolves to prevent them from doing so. Using this knowledge, drug developers will eventually be able to develop new anti-infective medications that prevent pathogens from penetrating host cells. Investigators hope that strengthening the host's defenses, rather than attacking the pathogens directly, will provide therapies against infectious disease that are more durable over the long term than those offered by antibiotics.

Pathogens and Their Hosts

Organisms have always been attacked by pathogens; the species that have survived, including us, are those that have evolved means to fend off their attacks. Likewise, pathogens have developed means to overcome these protective measures, forcing the evolution of even more powerful host defenses. Over millions of years, the arms race between pathogenic organisms and animals eventually created the mammalian immune system, which includes a wide variety of highly specialized compounds (toxic proteins that attack foreign cells marked with antibodies) as well as immune cells—the large macrophages of the blood and lymph, the natural killer cells, T lymphocytes and antibody-producing B lymphocytes. Immune cells patrol the bloodstream, various organ tissues, the surfaces of the intestines, and the respiratory and urinary tracts.

No matter where a pathogen comes from—via the respiratory or the digestive tract, an injury or an insect bite—it faces an army of immune cells that are specialized to devour invading pathogens, shower them with toxic chemicals, punch holes into their cell membranes or bombard them with antibodies to mark them for destruction. In fact, this defense system is so effective that most people spend most of their lives free of infectious disease, despite daily exposure to countless viruses, bacteria, and infectious eukaryotic parasites (microorganisms with nucleated cells, such as *Plasmodium*, the protozoan that causes malaria).

But pathogens, having the advantage of larger numbers, can overwhelm the host's immune system and often adapt more nimbly. Mutation and selection have provided them with mechanisms for circumventing or countering the immune system's attacks. Many pathogens, notably viruses but also many bacteria and eukaryotic microorganisms, invade host cells as a first step so that they are hidden from the immune system as they multiply. However, invasion is not a one-sided process; it often requires the active participation and cooperation of the host. The properties of both host and pathogen determine whether the pathogen can successfully establish an infection or whether it is killed by the host.

Invasion: Getting In

The immune system can detect alien organisms only outside cells or on the cell surface. This leaves the system vulnerable to attack from within its own cells. For instance, *Shigella flexneri*, a bacterium that infects people through feces-contaminated food and causes severe diarrhea and vomiting, first attaches to and then penetrates *macrophages*—immune cells that are specialized in devouring invading pathogens—as they patrol the intestines. *Shigella* multiplies inside the host cell, where it is unchallenged by the immune system. Eventually, the infected macrophage dies and releases new bacteria that spread to and infect nearby epithelial cells and cause destruction of the intestinal tissue. *Listeria monocytogenes*, a bacterium that causes meningitis and spontaneous abortion in pregnant women, first infects epithelial cells in the intestinal tract as it is taken up with contaminated food. The bacteria multiply and cross the epithelium to the bloodstream. It is in the blood that they penetrate the patient's immune cells, which then carry the infection all over the body. If those infected cells get into the brain and release the *Listeria*, they can cause meningitis, a life-threatening infection of the brain's surrounding membrane. If the infected cells travel through the placenta of a pregnant woman and release the pathogen in the fetus, the subsequent infection can kill the unborn child.

Another natural target is the lining of cells on the surface of the intestines or the lungs, another of the body's natural barriers against infectious microorganisms. All surfaces that are exposed to the outside—the skin, the intestines, the respiratory, and urinary tracts—are lined with epithelial cells that are so tightly interconnected that no virus or bacterium can squeeze through. In addition, these surfaces are covered with immune cells ready to attack any invading alien structure. Many pathogens therefore infect these cells first to establish a bridgehead from which they can release their progeny into the tissues and blood vessels that lie on the other, inner side of the epithelial barrier. The bloodstream may then become the medium through which they can spread throughout the body and infect other tissues and organs.

Pathogens have evolved a wide variety of mechanisms and strategies that enable them to enter body cells. However, a pathogen's invasion of a target cell often requires the active participation of the host. Indeed, the internalization of a pathogen involves the concerted interplay of many bacterial and host-cell proteins, and also involves the plasma membrane, the outer membrane that surrounds the host cell. The challenge for a pathogen, similar to the problem faced by a burglar cracking a safe, is to find a chemical code that starts the processes that eventually lead to its internalization by the host cell.

Pushing the Right Buttons

Internalization begins when the invading germ attaches to the host cell's plasma membrane and triggers the host cell to wrap its membrane around the invader.

Eventually, when the pathogen is completely wrapped up by the cell membrane, this structure buds off to form a membrane-coated vesicle with the virus, bacterium, or other microorganism inside. *Listeria* attaches to its target by displaying a so-called InlA (internalin) protein on its surface. InlA is specialized in making contact with a protein called E-cadherin on the surface of epithelial cells in the intestines. This initial contact triggers the movement of other host-cell surface proteins to the binding site; these reinforce the binding of the bacterium to the epithelial cell and help to stimulate the cytoskeleton. Another protein on *Listeria*'s surface, InlB, contacts two surface receptors on the host cell, which in turn activate an enzyme called PI3-kinase in the cell. PI3-kinase starts a series of events in the cell, which eventually induce the changes in the cytoskeleton that are necessary to internalize the attached bacterium. Indeed, this enzyme plays a key role in the *Listeria* infection process; experiments with an inhibitor of PI3-kinase have shown that the bacterium is unable to enter the cell if the enzyme cannot be activated.

An important factor in this process is the *cytoskeleton*, a scaffold of various proteins in the cell that define and maintain the cell's form. It is the cytoskeleton that performs the initial ruffling of the plasma membrane and the subsequent changes needed to wrap the membrane around the pathogen. This is an intricate process, so an invading pathogen has to manipulate the host cell's biochemical machinery considerably to induce its internalization. This task is performed by specialized molecules on the bacterium's surface that attach to specific receptor molecules on the host cell's surface. These receptors are molecular switches that react to specific molecules in the outer medium and induce metabolic changes within the cell. By pressing the right buttons, sending the right signals to the target cell, an invading pathogen can thus start the necessary events in the host cell's interior.

Many viruses use similar mechanisms to get into their target cells. The human immunodeficiency virus (HIV) that causes AIDS, for instance, first attaches to several proteins on the host cell's surface, triggering its internalization. After the virus has been taken up by the cell, its hull dissolves and releases the virus's genetic material, which is used by the host cell's bio-chemical machinery to produce more virus particles.

Several other bacteria have developed an even more sophisticated mechanism for forcing entry into the host cell. They carry needle-like structures on their surface through which they inject into the host cell proteins that eventually trigger internalization of the bacterium. *Shigella flexneri* uses this mechanism, called a type III secretion system, to inject two proteins that interact with signal-transduction proteins and the host cell's cytoskeleton. The activation of those proteins finally results in the reorganization of the cytoskeleton and the formation of ruffles in the plasma membrane required to internalize the pathogen.

A variation of this process, called *phagocytosis*, is actually used as a defense mechanism against invading bacteria. Some immune cells, and also epithelial cells in the intestines and the respiratory tract, engulf invading pathogens, take them up and digest them by breaking them down into their constituents. In particular, macrophages are specialized in destroying pathogenic bacteria through this process. Yet some pathogens, such as *Listeria* or the plague-causing *Yersinia pestis*, are able to manipulate phagocytosis so that they survive.

For those pathogens, it is important to stop the machinery eventually leading to their digestion. When a macrophage engulfs a cell, the result is a newly created vesicle called a *phagosome*. The phagosome fuses with a *lysosome*, another vesicle that contains a high concentration of digestive enzymes specialized in breaking down biological molecules. Several pathogens, such as the tuberculosis-causing *Mycobacterium tuberculosis*, the leprosy-causing *Mycobacterium leprae* or *Legionella pneumophila*, the cause of Legionnaires' disease, have been shown to prevent or slow down the fusion of the phagosome with the lysosome. The ability to redirect the phagosome pathway is presumably important for their survival and replication in the infected cell.

Nurturing the Parasite

The infection of a cell allows pathogens to take over the cell's biochemical machinery and produce offspring by using the nutrients that it finds in the host cell. Eventually, the production requires the delivery of additional nutrients at a rate that far exceeds the normal demand of a noninfected cell. Thus the pathogen has to manipulate the host cell's transport systems in the plasma membrane, not only to allow for this additional uptake of nutrients, but also to dispose of waste products that accumulate through the intense activity.

This manipulation is particularly obvious during the infection of red blood cells by the malaria-causing protozoan *Plasmodium*. Before infection, an erythrocyte is little more than a sack of hemoglobin proteins with a very low need for nutrients. Its membrane mainly contains transporter proteins that exchange bicarbonate ions, HCO_3-, with the surrounding medium and maintain the cell volume through the exchange of other ions. Since the cell does not synthesize proteins, DNA, or membranes, it has no need for amino acids, nucleic acids, lipids, vitamins, and so forth. The replicating malaria pathogen, however, has an excessive requirement for all these nutrients. Furthermore, to fuel the replication process, *Plasmodium* needs large amounts of glucose; indeed, an infected erythrocyte takes up 40 to 100 times more glucose than a noninfected cell.

To gain access to the necessary nutrients, *Plasmodium* forces the host cell to alter the transport properties of its membrane by inducing the so-called *new permeability pathway*. The pathogen forces the infected cell to activate additional transport proteins in its plasma membrane that carry sugars, nucleic acids, membrane components, and other substances from the intercellular medium into the cell. The necessity of the new permeability pathway for *Plasmodium*'s survival and replication is illustrated by the fact that several inhibitors of this pathway eventually kill the pathogen while it still remains in the erythrocyte.

The essential nature of the new permeability pathway is not yet clear and is being intensely studied.

Theoretically, the pathogen could express the respective transport systems itself and insert the proteins into the host-cell membrane. The advantage of this approach is that *Plasmodium* would not depend for its survival on the presence of adequate host-cell membrane proteins. The disadvantage, however, is that its proteins would be exposed at the membrane and thus would be recognized as alien structures by antibodies. Using the antibodies as markers, immune cells would sweep in and destroy the infected cell and the pathogen in it.

Alternatively, *Plasmodium* could modify existing host-cell membrane proteins to turn them into the new permeability pathway. The advantage of this mechanism is that the cell would remain undetected by the immune system. Indeed, recent experiments indicate that at least part of the new permeability pathway results from modification of existing cell-membrane proteins by the pathogen. Because *Plasmodium* depends on creation of the new permeability pathway to proliferate in the infected cell, investigators are hoping to find new malaria drugs to block this pathway. There is little doubt that other pathogens that rapidly proliferate inside infected host cells have to modify the transport properties of these cells in order to gain access to nutrients. But not much is known so far about the changes in nutrient transport that these pathogens induce in their host cells.

Opposing Forces

As we mentioned above, penetration of the host cell depends not only on the properties of the pathogen but also on the properties of the host. Some individuals have assets that protect their cells from being infected by certain pathogens. Most important to an appropriate defense is the ability of the immune system to kill pathogens before they enter host cells. Consequently, older people with a weaker immune system, as well as patients with an impaired immune system—HIV patients or people with an organ transplant who have to take immunosuppressive medication to suppress rejection of the transplanted organ—are more vulnerable to infectious diseases. Also, the immune system's ability to "remember" pathogens and to mount a faster and stronger defense in case of reinfection confers a strong advantage over time. Young children are particularly vulnerable to many diseases because their immune system is encountering the invading pathogen for the first time.

In addition, some people may be more or less resistant to some pathogens because of their genetic makeup. For instance, a certain mutation in a gene that carries the information for a receptor protein on the surface of white blood cells renders people partly or fully resistant to HIV. HIV uses this protein to attach to and infect white blood cells; the mutation changes the properties of the receptor, so that HIV is less able to infect those cells. It is a rare mutation, but it will eventually become more common in Africa and South Asia because it gives a clear evolutionary advantage for individuals in those areas where AIDS is rampant.

Sickle cell disease is the result of a mutation that changes a single amino acid—swapping glutamate for valine—in hemoglobin, the oxygen-storing protein in red blood cells. A patient who receives this mutation from both parents is severely ill, because hemoglobin precipitates and deforms the erythrocytes as soon as it is deprived of oxygen. However, an individual who carries only one mutant allele does not suffer from the disease; rather, the mutation impedes the intracellular survival of *Plasmodium* when the person is exposed to the pathogen. It is not entirely clear how the mutated hemoglobin protects against malaria.

In any case, the malaria pathogen has apparently never been able to overcome this resistance through evolution. Thus, individuals carrying the mutation have better survival chances in those areas where malaria is endemic, particularly in Africa and Southeast Asia. As a result, the incidence of the sickle cell trait and of sickle cell disease is particularly high in those areas. Similarly, thalassemia and glucose-6 phosphate dehydrogenase deficiency confer some resistance to malaria. Again, those diseases are particularly frequent in malaria-infested areas.

Leaving the Infected Cell

However comfortable life in an infected host cell may be, invading pathogens must leave in order to spread to other cells or tissues. Many viruses and bacteria do this in a rather crude way, by destroying the plasma membrane. The host cell simply bursts, releasing the pathogens into the surrounding medium. This process eventually leads to partial destruction of the tissue, leaving in its wake the ruins of dead cells.

Other pathogens, among them many viruses, leave the cell by using a reversal of the initial integration process. New viruses produced by the host cell travel to the plasma membrane, where they are wrapped in a membrane vesicle that buds off into the surrounding tissue.

The sudden release of pathogens is particularly dramatic in the case of *Plasmodium*. All infected red blood cells rupture synchronously to release into the blood stream a large number of new pathogens, which infect other erythrocytes. This cycle is repeated every two to three days. *Plasmodium*'s proliferation creates toxic metabolic end products, which are released in the blood and cause the regular fever attacks that are typical of malaria.

Assisted Apoptosis

A few pathogens use a rather sophisticated approach to kill the infected cell: They trigger it to commit suicide. This process, called *apoptosis*, is not a sudden burst of the cell, but rather a controlled shutdown of the cell's biochemical machinery and disassembly of its constituents.

Apoptosis is not unique to infected cells, but is a normal process that can be triggered by a variety of stimuli, such as radiation or the stimulation of proteins on the cell's surface, such as the CD95 or the P2X7 receptors. Caspases, a family of enzymes that are specialized in cleaving proteins, play a key role in apoptosis. Once activated, caspases trigger further events in the cell that break down the DNA in the nucleus, switch off and disintegrate the mitochondria (the energy-producing cell organelles) and lead to a rearrangement of the surrounding plasma membrane. This chain of events finally causes the cell to shrink and decompose into smaller particles that are taken up and digested by macrophages in the vicinity. *Shigella* triggers apoptosis of the infected macrophage in order to gain access to the underlying tissue, from which it can spread to other cells. Also, the ability to drive macrophages to cell death can protect a pathogen from being killed by those cells. *Yersinia*, for example, induces apoptosis as a way to escape from a macrophage before being digested. In fact, *Yersinia* bacteria that are unable to trigger apoptosis because of a defective YopJ protein are unable to kill macrophages and are thus less virulent than *Yersinia* with an intact YopJ protein.

Bacteria may trigger apoptosis by injecting proteins via their type III secretion system into the target cell. For instance, some of the proteins that *Shigella* and *Salmonella* inject through the type III secretory system stimulate the host cell's caspase I proteins. *Yersinia*, the plague-causing bacterium, injects a protein called YopJ into the target cell to trigger its internalization. YopJ also inhibits certain signaling proteins in the host cell, which usually suppress apoptosis. The release of YopJ by the bacterium thus triggers suicide of the infected cell.

New Weapons Against Disease

But apoptosis of the host cell may also be of benefit for the host, since pathogens released from the dying cell might then be taken up by macrophages that would destroy the pathogen. By sacrificing itself, the infected cell thus protects the body from a further progression of the infection. For instance, infection with *Pseudomonas aeruginosa*, an opportunistic bacterium that infects people with cystic fibrosis, triggers apoptosis of infected epithelial cells. Epithelial cells infected with *Pseudomonas aeruginosa* express two proteins on their surface: the CD95 receptor and the corresponding CD95 ligand. The ligand binds to the receptor and triggers apoptotic death of the infected cell. Indeed, mutant mice that are not able to express either the CD95 receptor or the ligand are killed by this pathogen, whereas mice that are able to express both proteins easily overcome a *Pseudomonas aeruginosa* infection. By analogy, the P2X7 receptor is assumed to play an important role in the killing of cells infected with *Mycobacterium tuberculosis*.

Bacteria are increasingly becoming resistant to various antibiotics. Multi-drug-resistant tuberculosis is growing into a serious health problem in Russia. For people with impaired immune systems, multi-resistant infectious bacteria have become a life-threatening problem. As the efficacy of existing drugs against many diseases declines, it is becoming increasingly important to find new ways to fight infectious organisms.

Moreover, there is yet no cure for most viral diseases. AIDS is devastating the population and economies of many African and Asian countries. At the same time, drug resistance is aiding the resurgence of malaria in Southeast Asia and Western Africa.

By understanding the nature of the infectious process, drug developers in academia and industry will gain the necessary knowledge to develop new treatments.

These new approaches at fighting infections do not aim to kill the infecting pathogen as classical antibiotics do. If a pathogen can be prevented from entering and hiding in host cells, it will be visible to the immune system and thus killed by the body's own defense mechanisms. Pathogens are also less likely to evolve resistance to drugs that work this way. Treatments based on this concept include small molecules that block the surface structures that pathogens use to recognize and attach to target cells and block their ability to trigger internalization. The understanding of host-cell resistance can also open up new possibilities for treatment. A number of biotechnology companies have already developed anti-infectives and are testing their efficiency to prevent and cure bacterial infections in clinical trials.

Reprinted with permission from *American Scientist.*

Recall the billions of cells that make up the human body. Now imagine that your job is to find a virus hiding within only 100 of these cells. How would you even begin? This is the challenge that biologists face today from human immunodeficiency virus (HIV). Once inside a host, HIV quickly infects T lymphocytes and monocytes, integrating into their DNA. Most of the time, HIV actively replicates inside these cells to make many new viral particles, but in some cells HIV simply lurks in wait. The cells with inactive HIV, called reservoir cells, are the real

problem in HIV therapy. These cells are nearly impossible to find and kill with current drugs. This article highlights the newest discoveries in reservoir cell biology from leading HIV researchers including Suzanne Crowe of the Macfarlane Burnet Institute for Medical Research and Public Health in Melbourne, Australia; Roger Pomerantz of Thomas Jefferson University; Mario Stevenson of the University of Massachusetts Medical School; Hamer and Jerome Zack of the University of California, Los Angeles; and Thomas Hope of the University of Illinois at Chicago. You will see how these scientists have tried to kill reservoir cells and will learn how and why they have failed. —JL

"Playing Hide and Seek the Deadly Way"
by Mike May
The Scientist, February 2, 2004

By November 2003, 40 million people worldwide—5 million more than the year before—were infected with HIV. In 2003, three million died of AIDS, bringing the total number lost to the epidemic to nearly 32 million people, the size of the population of Canada.

This insidious disease continues to prove itself. When this virus turns on, modern medicine can attack and kill, but it cannot cure. HIV hides. It slips inside other cells and waits. It can wait in reservoirs for years, probably longer than a person would live after contracting HIV. So scientists are trying to lure this killer out of hiding, turn it on, and destroy it. So far, some latent virus persists no matter what physicians throw at it, because today's drugs cannot detect the hidden virus. Moreover, HIV does not just infect cells: It integrates into the host cell's chromosome and DNA.

"I think that HIV hides in every place that it can," says Dean Hamer of the National Cancer Institute, "and it's pretty clever at doing so." He points to evidence from France Pietri-Rouxel of the Cochin Institute in Paris that HIV might even hide in fat cells.[1] Mulling over all the reservoir possibilities, Hamer concludes: "I would say any cell that's living and breathing and has CD4 is a target for HIV."

Scientists have found the virus in macrophages, monocytes, dendritic cells, and of course, CD4 + T cells. Finding every place that HIV hides, however, depends on how adept scientists become at uncovering it. Today's method's can find almost any amount of HIV; the problem is learning how to eradicate it. It may be that HIV cannot be wiped out. "It's like most of internal medicine," says Roger Pomerantz of Thomas Jefferson University in Philadelphia. "We don't cure much of anything." Diabetes, heart disease, and hepatitis, like HIV, all remain uncured. Some scientists think that defeating HIV will demand a new approach.

A Sad Tale

What they do know is that HIV binds to CD4 receptors on the surface of T lymphocytes. The infected T cells work as virus factories for HIV, which soon kills the cells. With enough T cells destroyed, a person cannot mount an immune response, so almost anything foreign, such as a bacterium, fungus, or another virus, poses a serious threat. The person infected with HIV usually dies from such opportunistic infections. Ongoing work, however, reveals many more players, making elimination of this virus an immense challenge.[2]

To keep track of the HIV infection, scientists measure the amount of viral mRNA in patients' plasma. Modern clinical techniques can detect as few as 50 copies of mRNA per milliliter; smaller amounts are considered undetectable. Moreover, the well-known drug regimen HAART (highly active antiretroviral therapy) can reduce HIV to 50 copies of less in many patients. When asked if HIV could be maintained at low levels and provide good outcomes for patients, the University of Barcelona's José Gatell replies, "This has been clearly demonstrated, at least for limited periods of time, six years." He adds, "Any potent regimen of HAART can achieve this goal, if the tolerance is reasonably good and the compliance to prescribed medication is above 90 percent to 95 percent."

If a patient goes off HAART though, the virus resurfaces, sometimes rebounding in just one week to pre-drug levels or higher. Some HIV probably remains in the blood; so if just one copy lingers, it rushes into reproduction as soon as HAART stops. And then there are the reservoirs, the places where HIV replicates little or not at all, going unnoticed by HAART. Those reservoirs have been found to cover more ground than was expected.

Taking the Pulse

Scientists have turned most often to T cells as the reservoir source, not only because HIV attacks T cells, but also because the T cells' normal function makes them possible reservoirs. Says Mario Stevenson of the University of Massachusetts Medical School, "There's a T cell that is essentially in a dormant state. It's called a quiescent T cell." Those cells remember past infections and mobilize rapidly if the same infection returns. Otherwise, this T cell sits and waits for years, even decades, mostly in tissues and lymph nodes.

Strategies to Reduce Latent Reservoirs of HIV

The first step is to induce the expression of the quiescent HIV genome in latently infected resting CD4 T cells using agents that activate transcription from the viral promoter. This is done in the presence of antiretroviral drugs (HAART) to prevent spreading infection by newly synthesized virus. The second step is to destroy the HIV+ cells, either by action of the virus itself, through the immune system, or by chimeric toxins that recognize the viral envelope glycoprotein Env present on the surface of infected cells.

That long life creates a problem when it involves HIV. If HIV finds its way into a quiescent T cell, then it should be able to live there for decades. (HIV kills cells, but not the quiescent T cells.) Instead, Stevenson says, "The popular theory is that a quiescent cell is in a state of dormancy. So when HIV gets in a cell that enters dormancy, HIV goes into dormancy along with it." Scientists can study HIV-infected, resting T cells and not find virus. But, if they stimulate those T cells so they become turned on, HIV starts replicating. "Basically, the virus has its finger on the pulse of the T cell," says Stevenson.

The T-cell reservoir could be very small, maybe as few as 100 cells. Nonetheless, experiments from Robert Siliciano's lab at the Johns Hopkins University School of Medicine put the half-life of those cells at about four years. It could take 60 years of HAART to eliminate all the virus hiding in the T-cell reservoir.[3] Even worse, the reservoir is not limited to T cells.

Of Monocytes and Macrophages

Dormant cells are not the only places where researchers are having a tough time drawing out the HIV virus. Other white blood cells, the monocytes, also play a role in HIV. Suzanne Crowe of the Macfarlane Burnet Institute for Medical Research and Public Health in Melbourne, Australia, explains that monocytes in the blood can be considered as members of two populations.[4] Two surface antigens, CD14 and CD16, distinguish the monocyte populations. One group expresses lots of CD14 proteins on its surface and very few CD16 proteins. These monocytes comprise most of the population, and tend to resist HIV infection. The other segment sports few CD14 proteins on its surface but many CD16s; this latter group expresses a receptor called CCR5, which binds HIV.

To explore this further, Crowe and her colleagues collected monocytes from HIV-infected patients. Then, the scientists divided the monocytes into two populations, one high in CD16 and one high in CD14. Crowe says, "Preliminary data show that the monocytes high in CD16 are more susceptible to HIV infection both in vivo, in blood from infected patients, as well as . . . in vitro." Moreover, the high-CD16 monocytes may go places that the other population cannot easily reach, such as the brain. So, the high CD16 monocytes could get infected with HIV and then hide where drugs may not go, contributing to the HIV reservoir problem.

As monocytes mature, they become macrophages, living for about two weeks in some tissues. But they may survive for months—maybe decades—in other places, including the brain. HIV-infected macrophages turn up in the brain, lung, lymph nodes, and spleen. Worse still, macrophages makes lots of virus. Even if infected T cells outnumber the infected macrophages by as much as 100-fold, it does not ensure that the T cells produce most of the virus. Because the infected macrophages do not become dormant like a resting T cell, the macrophages keep producing virus.

Master of the Game

HIV hides in many places. Once it crosses the body wall, HIV quickly invades quiescent T cells and these cells slip away to tissues and lymph nodes. HIV also infects monocytes, which may hide in various organs, including the brain. As monocytes mature they make macrophages, which also can be infected.

Monocytes also make dendritic cells which help the immune system recognize foreign antigens. Dendritic cells show up at every possible entry point: the oral cavity, intestine, vagina and rectum, where they pick up foreign particles and present them to T cells and B cells, eliciting an immune response.

HIV-infected dendritic cells pose real trouble. Thomas Hope of the University of Illinois at Chicago and his colleagues studied the interaction between HIV-infected dendritic cells and T cells.[5] By using time-lapse microscopy, Hope watched dendritic cells come into contact with T cells. In one experiment, HIV was distributed evenly over a dendritic cell before contact. Then, as the dendritic cell spread out over a T cell, the HIV moved to the place where the two cells first touched. In addition, a series of HIV receptors, including CD4, CCR5, and CXCR4, on the T cell also moved to that site. So, when a dendritic cell contacts a T cell, the HIV virus and its receptors become correctly positioned for a transfer to occur.

No matter how much the HIV moves around, finding it depends first on very sensitive tests, and those already exist. Says the University of Minnesota's Ashley Haase: "If you had a single copy of the virus in a cell, you could certainly detect it. The problem is really sampling." For example, he points out that 60 percent of the secondary lymph system is in the gut, and that covers a lot of area. "You might hit something, you might not." From extensive sampling, Haase concludes that T cells, monocytes, and macrophages hold the majority of the latent HIV. He agrees that dendritic cells hold some virus, too. Nonetheless, he adds, "Most of us think that most of the latently infected cells are resting CD4+ T cells."

Some Experimental Therapies

With HAART, clinicians can kill HIV in active cells, but the dormant cells cause the worst treatment problems. In one attempt to attack the HIV reservoir, Pomerantz and his colleagues studied three HIV-infected men who had been on HAART for more than a year. These men had no detectable virus in their blood samples, meaning fewer than 50 copies per milliliter of plasma.[6] Then, Pomerantz gave these patients two drugs, didanosine and hydroxyurea, which knock down viral replication even in resting cells, and two other drugs, OKT3 (an anti-CD3 monoclonal antibody) and interleukin-2, to turn on resting T cells. This treatment cut the viral load to less than one copy per milliliter. Every indicator showed no virus in these patients, so Pomerantz offered them drugless trials. "The good point," Pomerantz says, "is that they lasted significantly longer than the usual seven to 10 days before they rebounded. One lasted six months. Two rebounded after six weeks, which is still much, much longer, but they all came back. So we got close, but we didn't get it to zero."

Hamer and Jerome Zack of the David Geffen School of Medicine at the University of California, Los Angeles, put together a research team to try another tactic, immunotoxins.[7] The immuno component of their immunotoxin recognized a specific glycoprotein in the envelope of HIV, and the Pseudomonas toxin in the compound killed any cell with that glycoprotein. They tested this treatment on an SCID-hu mouse, which incorporates human liver and thymus cells to make a mouse that creates human T cells; this animal has no immune system of its own. Then, Hamer and Zack infected these mice with HIV. Next, they treated infected cells with the immunotoxin and interleukin-7, which should turn on viral expression but not affect uninfected cells. In comparison to cells treated with the immunotoxin alone, the combination therapy reduced the new virus production by 70 percent and reduced virus-producing cells by 50 percent. Says Zack: "We used a minimum activation signal that didn't affect the phenotype or function of normal cells, but it still turned on the latent cells." Despite the power of this approach, some virus survived.

In short, the HIV reservoir escapes virtually all available therapies. Anthony S. Fauci, director of the National Institute of Allergy and Infectious Diseases, says, "A number of studies throughout the years—from our lab, from Robert Siliciano's lab, from other labs—have indicated that, despite the suppression of virus replication for up to several years with antiretroviral therapies, when you look for the reservoir, you inevitably find it, virtually without exception. And when you discontinue the drug, in most everybody with very few exceptions, the virus bounces back." As a result, HIV currently demands a course of antiretroviral therapy that continues indefinitely, but that, too, might fail.

Other Strategies

Instead of looking only to drug treatments, some scientists look at the human immune system itself: Perhaps HAART could reduce the virus, and then the immune system could clean up what's left. For example, a nucleic-acid-editing enzyme called APOBEC3G is made inside HIV-infected cells. This enzyme deactivates viruses by changing the nucleic acids in the viral DNA. In HIV, APOBEC3G converts cytosine to uracil in the viral DNA that is generated during reverse transcription, thereby blocking further infection.

Deadly Recruitment

The question is whether the localization of HIV particles was altered when dendritic cells were observed shortly after contact with adherent, CD4-positive cells. The answer is yes. In the first frame, the virus was evenly distributed throughout both dendritic cells. Within six minutes, the cell in the top of the frame began to spread out on target, and the majority of HIV relocated to the initial site of contact. The researchers observed movement in the other cell at 18 minutes. In both cells, the majority of the particles moved within one, three-minute time frame.

Nevertheless, "HIV almost never gets killed by APOBEC3G," emphasizes Didier Trono of the University of Geneva.[8] "Instead, APOBEC3G edits the genome of the virus a little bit, which makes HIV even harder to fight." Trono's group analysed one variant of APOBEC3G that apparently leads to a faster progression of AIDS. "We found this variant slightly more active," Trono says. "It might accelerate disease progression by inducing a faster genetic drift for HIV because of a stronger APOBEC3G." Instead of APOBEC3G helping in the fight against HIV, it might make it worse. "This antiviral factor and its interplay with HIV probably contributes to the reservoir's diversity and difficulty to track down," says Trono.

To get a better view of how HIV works, perhaps scientists need to work less in vitro and more in vivo. Several years ago, Haase and his colleagues discovered that the resting T cells produce some virus, but this appears only in vivo, not in tissue culture.[9] To explore the very beginning of HIV infection, he turned to the simian immunodeficiency virus found in monkeys. "When the virus first enters a host," Haase says, "it does not see lots of activated T cells. It sees many resting T cells. In contrast to a lot of people, I think the latent cells get infected very early on." Haase says he believes that the virus goes into a reservoir right away. Moreover, his work shows that even the reservoir replicates a small amount of virus. "It's diabolical," Haase says. The reservoir reproduces just enough to trigger an immune response that helps the HIV infect activated T cells, where the virus replicates most efficiently.

HIV continues to slip out of every trap that scientists create. "What we know," concluded Stevenson last year, "represents only a thin veneer on the surface of what needs to be known."

References

1. U. Hazen *et al.*, "Human adipose cells express CD4, CXCR4, and CCR5 receptors: a new target cell type for the immunodeficiency virus-1?" *FASEB J*, 16:1254-6, 2002.
2. M. Stevenson, "HIV-1 pathogenesis," *Nat Med*, 9:853-60, 2003.
3. D. Finizi et al., "Latent infection of CD4(+) T cells provides a mechanism for lifelong persistence of HIV-1, even in patients on effective combination therapy," *Nat Med*, 5:512-7, 1999.
4. S. Crowe, "The contribution of monocyte infection and trafficking to viral persistence, and maintenance of the viral reservoir in HIV infection," *J Leukoc Biol*, 74:635-41, 2003.
5. D. McDonald *et al.*, "Recruitment of HIV and its receptors to dendritic cell-T cell junctions," *Science*, 300:1295-7, 2003.
6. J. Kulkosky *et al.*, "Intensification and stimulation therapy for human immunodeficiency virus type 1 reservoirs in infected persons receiving

virally suppressive highly active antiretroviral therapy," *J Infect Dis*, 186:1403-11, 2002.

7. D. Brooks *et al.*, "Molecular characterization, reactivation, and depletion of latent HIV," *Immunity*, 19:413-23, 2003.

8. B. Mangeat *et al.*, "Broad antiretroviral defense by human APOBEC3G through lethal editing of nascent reverse transcripts," *Nature*, 424:21-2, 2003.

9. T. Schacker *et al.*, "Productive infection of T cells in lymphoid tissues during primary and early human immunodeficiency virus infection," *J Infect Dis*, 183:555-62, 2001.

Anthrax, a bacterial disease, is a potential biological weapon. Infection with Bacillus anthracis can sometimes be fought with antibiotics, but it is also important to counter the effects of anthrax toxins. This article summarizes the work of two prominent anthrax biologists: Dr. John A. T. Young, professor at the Salk Institute for Biological Studies, and Dr. Robert Liddington, professor at the University of Leicester. During infection, an anthrax protein called protective antigen binds to a receptor on human cells. Dr. Young's group has identified precisely which receptor it is, which could aid efforts to design drugs to prevent the receptor from joining with the protective antigen. After the protective antigen binds to the cell receptor, it is cleaved, or cut, by a human protease. The cleaved protective antigen binds to two anthrax proteins: lethal factor and

oedema factor. The whole complex of proteins is then taken inside the host cell, where lethal factor and oedema factor can wreak havoc. Dr. Liddington's laboratory has discovered the detailed molecular structure of lethal factor. With this knowledge, scientists may be able to devise drugs that bind to lethal factor, keeping it away from the protective antigen and thereby keeping it from exerting its toxic effects. —JL

"Tackling Anthrax"
by Arthur M. Friedlander
Nature, November 8, 2001

In 1990, during the Gulf War, and then again in 1998, the decision was made to vaccinate US military personnel against the possible use of anthrax as a biological weapon. Never before had vaccinations been carried out as a response to anything but the natural occurrence of a disease. Now, spores of the causative bacterium, *Bacillus anthracis*, are being used to kill civilians and create panic: the question of how to deal with anthrax has shot straight to the top of the medical agenda.

There are three ways to tackle the disease: vaccination to prevent bacterial infection in the first place; antibiotics, to attack infection if it occurs; and anti-toxin treatments for the bacterium's toxic effects. Papers by Bradley *et al.*[1] and Pannifer *et al.*[2] will help in developing the last approach. The possible emergence of antibiotic- and vaccine-resistant organisms[3] adds further impetus to the search for new approaches to preventing or treating anthrax.

The existence of toxins of *B. anthracis* was postulated by Robert Koch in the nineteenth century, when he discovered the cause of anthrax. Since their subsequent discovery almost 50 years ago, the toxins (known as 'lethal' and 'oedema'), along with the capsule that surrounds the bacterium, have been recognized as the main components that enable anthrax to cause harm. However, the manifestations of anthrax infection are not solely due to the effects of the toxins, as is the case with diphtheria, tetanus, or botulism.

Rather, in anthrax the bacterium invades and grows to high concentrations in the host; the toxins act mainly by damaging defensive cells called phagocytes, causing the immune system to malfunction. Late in the infection, toxins may be present in large amounts in the blood and contribute directly to the death of the infected organism. Some studies, in non-human primates, suggest that lethal toxin by itself is not even particularly potent, requiring milligram quantities to cause death. But the results of other work,[4] in mice, imply that further non-toxin components contribute to virulence that have yet to be identified. So antibiotics constitute the mainstay of treatment, although anti-toxins have long been considered[5] an essential 'adjunctive' therapy, and remain so.

The toxins are composed of three proteins: a cell-receptor binding protein, known as protective antigen; and two enzymes, lethal factor and oedema factor. The papers by Bradley *et al.*[1] and Pannifer *et al.*[2] respectively report on the identity of the cellular receptor for protective antigen, and the crystal structure of lethal factor. This valuable information about the toxins will allow the identification of vulnerable targets for anti-toxin therapy.

Lethal factor is a zinc protease, a type of enzyme that contains zinc and cleaves other proteins. Oedema factor belongs to a class known as adenylate cyclases. When combined with lethal factor, protective antigen constitutes lethal toxin; with oedema factor it makes oedema toxin. From cell-culture studies it seems that anthrax operates as follows. First, protective antigen is cleaved, and so activated, by a protease on the surface of the cell under attack. It then forms heptamers—aggregations of seven—and subsequently binds one or more molecules of lethal or oedema factor, or both. The complex passes into the cell through the receptor for protective antigen and on into an acidic compartment inside the cell. There the heptamer inserts into the compartment's membrane, releasing lethal and oedema factors into the cell body where they exert their toxic effects. The precise molecular targets remain unknown.

Several features of these events remain unclear, such as the ratios of molecules in the complex between protective antigen and lethal and oedema factors, and whether both factors are included. A protease in the blood stream can also activate protective antigen, and complexes with lethal factor occur in the blood of infected animals. So the relative importance of the two proteases in toxin action *in vivo* is unknown.

The structure of lethal factor[2] will help in the identification of drugs that interfere with its binding, and maybe that of oedema factor, to protective antigen; indeed, such a peptide inhibitor has been described.[6] Investigating inhibitors of the activities of the two factors themselves is another route, and will be aided by knowledge of the crystal structures.[2] Therapies might include soluble toxin receptors and other drugs to prevent protective antigen from binding to its receptor. Non-toxic mutants of protective antigen have been shown to neutralize toxin,[7,8] and inhibitors of the protease(s) that activates it might have the same effect. Here, detailed knowledge of toxin kinetics during infection will be required, and the timing of drug delivery is critical. Another tactic may develop from understanding how a recently discovered motor protein confers resistance to lethal toxin in some phagocytes.[9]

Further adjunctive treatments might include antibodies to the toxin, spore, and bacillus. Other bacteria that cause sepsis exert pathological effects by triggering an inflammatory response from molecules known as cytokines; treatment with activated protein C has been reported[10] to be effective in such cases. The possible role of cytokines in anthrax warrants further evaluation, as do other ways of preventing the physiological consequences of the toxins. The extensive experience of testing adjunctive therapies for sepsis will be invaluable in guiding this work. In the current circumstances, however, priority should go to evaluating antibacterial drugs, initially antibiotics that have already been licensed for use.

Two final points are that information from sequencing of the B. anthracis genome, currently underway, may prove invaluable in tackling anthrax. And it is extraordinarily difficult to test anti-anthrax therapies in humans, so large clinical trials with non-human primates may well be needed.

In the early days of microbiology, 125 years ago, anthrax was significant mainly as an economically damaging disease of domesticated animals. The world's scientific community addressed that problem and developed effective countermeasures. It is now necessary once again to focus on anthrax, along with other pathogenic microorganisms, this time as agents of biological terrorism and threats to civilization. During the Second World War, the Office of Scientific Research and Development in the United States, and similar agencies in other countries, coordinated the application of science to warfare.[11] The same level of organization and commitment is needed today.

End Notes

1. Bradley, K. A., Mogridge, J., Mourez, M., Collier, R. J. & Young, J. A. T. *Nature* **414**, 225–229 (2001).

2. Pannifer, A. D. *et al. Nature* **414**, 229–233 (2001).

3. Pomerantsev, A. P. *et al. Vaccine* **15**, 1846–1850 (1997).

4. Welkos, S. L. *Microb. Pathogen.* **10**, 183–198 (1991).

5. Lincoln, R. E. & Fish, D. C. in *Microbial Toxins* (eds Montie, T. C., Kadis, S. & Ajl, S. J.) 361–414 (Academic, New York, 1970).

6. Mourez, M. *et al. Nature Biotechnol.* **19**, 958–961 (2001).

7. Sellman, B. R., Mourez, M. & Collier, R. J. *Science* **292**, 695–697 (2001).

8. Singh, Y., Khanna, H., Chopra, A. P. & Mehra, V. *J. Biol. Chem.* **276**, 22090–22094 (2001).

9. Watters, J. W., Dewar, K., Lehoczky, J., Boyartchuk, V. & Dietrich, W. F. *Curr. Biol.* **11**, 1503–1511 (2001).
10. Bernard, G. R. *et al. N. Engl. J. Med.* **344**, 699–709 (2001).
11. Singer, M. *Washington Post* A21 (24 September, 2001).

Bacteria are not always harmful to humans. In fact, without the bacteria that live in our intestines, we would lack several important nutrients and would be less able to fend off intestinal pathogens. Intestinal bacteria are called commensals, meaning that they live inside of another organism harmlessly. Some commensals in our gut are not only harmless, they actually benefit us; these are called symbionts. Yet, as Dr. Michael J. G. Farthing of St. George's Hospital Medical School in London shows, this arrangement sometimes turns sour. Commensals in the intestines occasionally cause unintentional harm, such as turning certain compounds into carcinogens during their metabolism processes. Even worse, many commensals can be turned into potent pathogens by picking up only a few "virulence factors," or genes that allow the bacteria to make toxins or attack the host. For example, E. coli made news several years ago when fast-food hamburgers tainted with the bacteria caused food poisoning and even death. E. coli actually live in great numbers in our gut quite harmlessly, *but as Dr. Farthing explains, one genetic addition can make them deadly. —JL*

"Bugs and the Gut: An Unstable Marriage"
by Michael J. G. Farthing, M.D., F.R.C.P
Best Practice and Research Clinical Gastroenterology

There is a symbiotic relationship between the gastrointestinal microflora and the human host. Commensal bacteria provide essential nutrients to the epithelium and promote healthy immune responses in the gut. Commensal bacteria such as *Escherichia coli* can, however, transform into pathogens when they acquire genetic material encoding virulence factors such as adhesins, enterotoxins, invasins, and cytotoxins.

Enterovirulent organisms "communicate" with the host by a variety of diverse mechanisms; these underpin the pathogenic processes that are essential for the expression of diarrhoeal disease. Many of these mechanisms involve the activation of signal transduction pathways in epithelial cells. Classical pathways include activation of adenylate or guanylate cyclases to produce chloride secretion, and subversion of cytoskeletal functions to effect intimate attachment with or without invasion of epithelial cells. Other systems are also involved, including inflammatory cells and local neuroendocrine networks.

Understanding the complex interactions between the human gastrointestinal tract and the commensals and pathogens which it encounters will hopefully help us to exploit further the beneficial effects of the "marriage" and to find new ways of preventing and treating microbial disease of the intestine which occurs when the symbiotic arrangement breaks down.

Commensals and Pathogens

The human and its gastrointestinal microflora are inextricably linked. This association between man and alimentary tract microbes is presumed to have occurred at the earliest stages of human evolution. About 10^{14} bacteria inhabit the human alimentary tract, which is about tenfold greater than the total number of host eukaryote cells in the human organism.[1] For the bacterial prokaryote, the human alimentary tract offers a relatively non-hostile environment and a plentiful supply of nutrients. The luminal milieu along the tract varies with environmental niches for aerobic, facultatively anaerobic and anaerobic organisms. Likewise, the human host benefits from products of bacterial metabolism such as short-chain fatty acids (SCFAs), and also from the important contributions that the bacterial flora make to immune and non-immune host defence.[2]

However, not all bacteria in the alimentary tract are friendly. Closely related organisms can be both commensal and pathogen, the switch being initiated by the presence of genetic material commonly localized in a region of the bacterial chromosome or within a plasmid. This so-called "pathogenicity island" or locus, encodes one or more virulence factors which are necessary for the expression of human disease. Overall, it would appear that virulent, disease-producing organisms are greatly outnumbered by their commensal cousins and that pathogenicity is therefore a relatively rare event. However, the emergence of virulent, disease-producing strains of enteric bacteria probably favours survival of the organism by ensuring transmission to other humans that would be facilitated by diarrhoeic stools.

Thus, the human organism is a eukaryote–prokaryote consortium with a high degree of inter-dependency. Just as the consortium is unlikely to have occurred by chance and without mutual advantage, it is also unlikely that mutual co-operation is achieved without some clear lines of communication. There is abundant evidence that there is sophisticated "cross-talk" between enteropathogens and the many cell systems that make up the gastrointestinal tract.[3,4] Enteropathogens have acquired molecular mechanisms to subvert host cytoskeletal components and signal transduction systems to colonize and create a favourable environment in the gut.[5, 6, 7] The lines of communication between commensal organisms and host cells are less well established, although there is good evidence that commensal bacteria influence epithelial cell turnover in the gut, drive the normal gut mucosal immune response and contribute a variety of essential nutrients to host epithelial cell metabolism.

The Origins of Symbiosis

Symbiosis is the peaceful and profitable coexistence between two organisms. Symbiosis in the intestine is an ancient phenomenon. Early humans appeared about 400 million years ago but the association between a prokaryotic microflora with the eukaryotic alimentary tract of animals began 1000–2000 million years ago. Symbiosis probably played an even more fundamental role in the evolution of eukaryotic cells which are believed to have developed by a process called serial endosymbiosis in which eukaryotic cells evolved as multiples of prokaryotes.[8] The typical bacterial prokaryote has a nucleoid (or genophore) and thus lacks a nucleus with nuclear membranes. In addition, it lacks mitochondria, large ribosomes and endoplasmic reticulum and has only a simple flagellum, unlike the more complex eukaryotic undulipodium. There is now compelling evidence that the eukaryotic nucleus evolved from endosymbiotic fermenting thermophilic eubacteria, that mitochondria originated from aerobic eubacteria, that internalized spirochaetes provided the motile cytoskeletal proteins that are vital for mitosis and meiosis and that other external spirochaetes formed the basis of the eukaryotic undulipodium; hence, the basic eukaryotic cell was formed from a series of prokaryotic "add-ons."[8] More recently an alternative biochemically based hypothesis, the "hydrogen hypothesis" has been put forward to explain the transition from pro- to eukaryotic state.[9] The hypothesis, however, is still dependent on the principle of symbiosis, and suggests that the host (an anaerobic, strictly hydrogen-dependent, autotrophic archaebacterium) became associated with a eubacterium symbiont that was able to respire, but generated hydrogen as a waste product of anaerobic heterotrophic metabolism. It is proposed that the host's dependence on molecular hydrogen acted as a selective principle for the emerging eukaryotic state.

Thus, whatever theory is eventually shown to be the most likely explanation for this aspect of cellular evolution, human evolution has from the earliest times been totally dependant on prokaryotic endosymbiosis and even today continues to rely on a symbiotic relationship with its enteric microflora.

The Gastrointestinal Microflora

More than 500 species of bacteria colonize the alimentary tract with marked regional differences both in the type of bacteria and the total number of organisms present.[10] All of the bacteria present in the gastrointestinal tract enter through the mouth either with food and drink or by direct person-to-person contact. The mouth has a unique flora containing aerobes and anaerobes. Although many bacteria are swallowed every day, the low intragastric pH restricts bacterial numbers in gastric fluid (10^3/ml), most of which are lactobacilli. *Helicobacter pylori* has resided in the human stomach for about 300 million years and for longer in some small mammals and other animals. It is suggested that *H. pylori* can function as both a commensal (and possibly even a symbiont) and a pathogen.[11] In the duodenum bacterial numbers rise to 10^4/ml and, as in the stomach, these bacteria are predominantly lactobacilli. There is a sharp rise in the distal ileum to 10^6 organisms/ml, with streptococci appearing in addition to the lactobacilli. In the caecum, bacterial counts rise markedly to 10^{12}/g faeces, with a major contribution by anaerobic organisms such as *Bacteroides*, *Clostridium*, and methanogenic bacteria.[12]

The gastrointestinal tract of the neonate is sterile but within hours it gradually becomes colonized by bacteria acquired from the mother and other environmental sources. The neonatal intestine contains predominantly lactobacilli and bifidobacteria, but after weaning the microflora begins to reflect more closely that of the adult.

The intestinal microflora plays a major role in the maintenance of mucosal structure.[12] Studies in germ-free animals have shown that establishment of a normal microflora increases mucosal mass, intestinal surface area, and epithelial cell turnover. These structural alterations almost certainly have functional implications with respect to nutrient, fluid, and electrolyte absorption and for epithelial regeneration and repair.

The gut microflora also makes an important contribution to host defence by promoting the establishment of a resident population of immunocytes and other inflammatory cells within the epithelium and lamina propria which is the front line of immune host defence against invading enteropathogens. There is now good evidence that the commensal microflora play a direct role in suppressing gut enteropathogens.[1]

Louis Pasteur noted the antagonism between certain bacterial strains while his colleague and professional sparing partner, Metchnikoff, proposed the possibility of using lactic-acid-producing bacteria therapeutically. There is now increasing evidence that the commensal microflora play a direct role in suppressing the colonization and proliferation of the gut by enteropathogens. Lactobacilli produce lactic acid and SCFAs that reduce intraluminal pH and inhibit the growth of acid-intolerant organisms. Bifidobacteria, a major commensal of the neonate, have been shown to reduce dramatically the risk of rotavirus infection in this age group.[13]

The concept of administering a harmless organism to prevent infection has become known as *probiotics*.[1] Attempts have also been made to use *prebiotics* that are dietary substrates such as fructose-containing oligosaccharides (found in large quantities of onions, carrots, and garlic) to promote the growth of resident probiotics such as bifidobacteria. Further work is required to determine whether this principle will find a place in clinical practice.

Commensals contribute to the nutritional status of the animal. The rumen of some herbivores contains a highly specialized microflora that is able to digest cellulose and other plant structural molecules, making them available to the host as energy substrates. In the human colon many bacterial species metabolize fibre and other unabsorbed carbohydrates to produce SCFAs. This liberates and allows retrieval of energy substrates that would otherwise be lost in the faeces. Butyrate, in particular, is an important fuel for the colonocyte for in addition to its direct effects on cell metabolism it may also have preventive effects against neoplasia.[14] Bacteria may also contribute directly to host nutritional status by synthesizing vitamins such as vitamin K and vitamin B^{12}.

The Normal Microflora Turns "Pathogen"

The intestinal microflora does not always have a positive effect on the host. Some intestinal bacteria are able to deconjugate bile salts. Fat malabsorption can result in conditions that promote bacterial overgrowth in the small intestine. This is due to reduced concentrations of conjugated bile salts and to the membranotoxic effects of unconjugated bile salts on the epithelium of the small intestine. The normal intestinal flora actively participates in the metabolic pathways of a variety of endogenous steroid hormones and in the excretion profiles of many drugs. Colonic bacteria with azoreductase activity are thought to be involved in the conversion of dietary pro-carcinogens to carcinogens in the intestine, thereby having a role in the pathogenesis of colorectal cancer.[15]

The presence of commensal microorganisms in the intestine is thought to be important in promoting the normal background inflammatory infiltrate which is a vital component of host immune defence. In certain circumstances, such as inflammatory bowel disease, the inflammatory response may get out of control with loss of immune tolerance to the normal microflora.[16] A similar situation may also exist in the tropics where some healthy individuals have mild or moderate partial villous atrophy, so-called tropical enteropathy. This may occur as a result of mucosal T cell activation driven either by the normal microflora (total bacterial counts are often increased compared to Western controls) or to repeated intestinal infection.[17] In immunodeficiency, harmless species such as *Candida albicans* can invade to produce chronic infection such as candida oesophagitis.

Transforming a Commensal Into a Pathogen

One of the most common bacterial species in the human alimentary tract is *Escherichia coli*. In healthy humans these organisms are harmless commensals and have a symbiotic relationship with the host. However, during the last 50 years a variety of sub-types have been characterized that are pathogenic to humans and animals which produce an extensive spectrum of clinical disease including acute watery diarrhoea, dysentery, and persistent diarrhoea sometimes with nutrient malabsorption. Although in each case the basic *E. coli* organism is fundamentally the same, the various pathogenic sub-types possess additional genetic material that encodes for specific virulence factors that directly determine the nature of the intestinal disease.[3,4] Enterotoxigenic *E. coli* (ETEC), for example, possess two major virulence factors, both plasmid-encoded. ETEC have highly specialized attachment organelles called pili which mediate adherence to host epithelium. These pili demonstrate selectivity in their binding characteristics in that human, porcine, and bovine *E. coli* adhere most efficiently to their natural host; they cause little or no disease in the other mammalian hosts. ETEC also possess genes that encode the secretory entero-toxins, heat-labile toxins I and II (LT-I, LT-II), and heat stable toxin (ST_a). Once ETEC has adhered to and colonized the small intestine these enterotoxins induce intestinal secretion by promoting chloride ion secretion from the epithelial cells of the small intestine.

Enteropathogenic *E. coli* (EPEC) and enterohaem-orrhagic *E. coli* (EHEC) have a pathogenicity locus that encodes several genes which enable these organisms first to attach to the intestinal epithelium and then to disrupt the brush border membrane, producing the so-called attaching/effacing lesion characteristic of these infections.[18,19] EHEC, in addition, has a chromosomal gene that encodes Shiga-like toxins I and II (SLT-I, SLT-II), which have close sequence homology to Shiga toxin and have similar inhibitory effects on protein synthesis.

These cytotoxins contribute to the inflammatory colitis that is characteristic of this infection.

Enteroinvasive *E. coli* (EIEC) differ from the other types of *E. coli* as they possess several surface proteins that permit direct invasion of the bacterium into the host epithelial cell. These invasion plasmid antigens (Ipa A–D) are identical to those found in Shigella sp.[20, 21, 22] making EIEC and *Shigella* close relatives both genetically and in the type of human disease that they produce.

Thus, the difference between *E. coli* as a commensal and a pathogen depends entirely on the presence of additional genetic material encoding one or more of a series of virulence factors. These virulence factors are often located together in pathogenicity loci, suggesting that, over time, they have moved together to endow previous commensals with a complete "pathogenicity package" or virulence cassette.

Identification of the many interactions that occur between a pathogen and its host is clearly central to the development of our understanding of the pathogenesis of disease, of immune and non-immune host defence mechanisms and, ultimately, to the establishment of new therapeutic and prevention strategies. Enteric pathogens use a variety of lines of communication by which they are able to secure a colonization niche within the intestine, techniques which often involve subversion of host intracellular signalling pathways and utilization of certain structural components of the host epithelial cell, particularly the cytoskeleton.[5,6] Bacterial communication strategies can be classified into four major types depending on the final location of the bacterium, namely: (i) the intestinal lumen, (ii) intimate adherence and disruption of the apical membrane of the enterocyte, (iii) invasion of the epithelium and sub-epithelial structures, and (iv) systemic effects either by direct penetration into the circulation or through the action of distant signalling molecules such as cytokines.

Although enteric pathogens have their primary interactions with the host epithelial cell or its specialized relative the M cell, which covers the dome of Peyer's patches, it is now increasingly clear that enteropathogens also engage in cross-talk through other endogenous lines of communication. These include the mucosal immune system, other inflammatory cells involved in host defence such as polymorphonuclear neutrophils and mast cells, and the enteric nervous system.

End Notes

1. Bengmark S. Ecological control of the gastrointestinal tract. *Gut* 1998; **42**:2–7.
2. Guarner F & Malagelada J-R. Gut flora in health and disease. *Lancet* 2003; **361**: 512–519.
3. Strauss EJ & Falkow S. Microbial pathogenesis: genomics and beyond. *Science* 1997; **276**: 707–712.
4. Finley BB & Falkow S. Common themes in microbial pathogenicity revisited. *Microbiology and Molecular Biology Reviews* 1997; **61**: 136–169.
5. Cossart P. Subversion of the mammalian cell cytoskeleton by invasive bacteria. *Journal of Clinical Investigation* 1997; **99**: 2307–2311.
6. Finlay BB & Cossart P. Exploitation of mammalian cell function by bacterial pathogens. *Science* 1997; **276**: 718–725.
7. Darwin KH & Miller VL. Molecular basis of the interaction of *Salmonella* with the intestinal mucosa. *Clinical Microbiology Review* 1999; **12**: 405–428.
8. Margulis L. *Serial Endosymbiosis Theory*, 2nd edn. Symbiosis in Cell Evolution, New York: Freeman, 1993. pp. 1–18.
9. Martin W & Müller M. The hydrogen hypothesis for the first eukaryote. *Nature* 1998; **392**: 37–41.
10. Tannock GW. Normal Microflora: an Introduction to Microbes Inhabiting the Human Body. London: Chapman and Hall, 1995.

11. Blaser MJ. Not all *Helicobacter pylori* strains are created equal: should all be eliminated? *Lancet* 1997; **349**: 1020–1022.

12. Heneghan JB. Alimentary tract physiology: interactions between the host and its microflora. In Rowland IR (ed.) *Role of the Gut Flora in Toxicity and Cancer*. London: Academic Press, 1988. pp. 39–77.

13. Saavedra JM, Bauman NA, Oung I *et al*. Feeding of *Bifidobacterium bifidum* and *Streptococcus thermophilus* to infants in hospital for prevention of diarrhea and shedding of rotavirus. *Lancet* 1994; **344**: 1046–1049.

14. Gibson PR, Kilias D, Rosella O *et al*. Effect of topical butyrate on rectal epithelial kinetics and mucosal enzyme activities. *Clinical Science* 1998; **94**: 671–676.

15. Mallett AK & Rowland IR. Factors affecting the gut microflora. In Rowland IR (ed.) *Role of the Gut Flora in Toxicity and Cancer*. London: Academic Press, 1988, pp. 347–382.

16. MacDonald TM. Breakdown of tolerance to the intestinal bacterial flora in inflammatory bowel disease (IBD). *Clinical and Experimental Immunology* 1995; **102**: 445–447.

17. Veitch AM, Kelly P, Zulu IS *et al*. Tropical enteropathy: a T cell-mediated crypt hyperplastic enteropathy. *European Journal of Gastroenterology and Hepatology* 2001; **13**: 1175-1181.

18. Kenny B, DeVinney R, Stein M *et al*. Enteropathogenic E. coli (EPEC) transfers its receptor for intimate adherence into mammalian cells. *Cell* 1997; **91**: 511–520.

19. Knutton S, Rosenshine I, Pallen MJ *et al*. A novel EspA-associated surface organelle of enteropathogenic Escherichia coli involved in protein translocation into epithelial cells. *EMBO Journal* 1998; **17**: 2166-2176.

20. Galan JE. Molecular genetics bases of Salmonella entry into host cells. *Molecular Microbiology* 1996; **20**:. 263-271.

21. Adam T, Giry M, Bowuet P & Sansonetti P. Rho-dependent membrane folding causes Shigella entry into epithelial cells. *EMBO Journal* 1996; **15**: 3315-3321.

22. Menard R, Prevost MC, Gounon P *et al*. The secreted Ipa complex of Shigella flexneri promotes entry into mammalian cells. Proceedings of the National Academy of Sciences of the USA 1996; **93**: 1254-1258.

4 What Are Viruses?

They are not alive in the strict sense of the term, but they can take over a living organism quickly. Viruses are crafted to infect cells and replicate rapidly. What's more, in order to confuse their host's immune system, viruses are primed to change. In this article, you will be introduced to the various steps of viral infection and replication. You will also learn the techniques viruses use to change and evolve. When humans began to domesticate animals, the close contact between species allowed different viruses to be in the same host at the same time. It seems that by exchanging parts of their genetic code, new and more infectious viruses were born. This is still true, as evidenced by the jump of diseases like HIV from monkeys to humans, or influenza from birds to humans. The DNA of viruses can also easily mutate when viruses replicate rapidly inside a host cell. Natural selection weeds out the defective viruses and allows the most effective versions to take over. All of these traits highlight the importance of biological research in viral infection and cellular defense, so scientists can develop new antiviral drugs to keep one step ahead of the changing foe. —JL

"The Living Dead"
by Patricia Davis
New Scientist, Oct. 13, 2001

Are viruses dead or alive? They are either the simplest life forms we know or the most complex, lifeless molecules on the planet. They use the genetic code common to all organisms, but outside the living cells they parasitise they are completely inert. What is certain is that their influence over life is mind-boggling.

Viruses are infectious particles that must invade living cells in order to replicate, often with disastrous consequences for the host organism. They can infect all organisms and, compared with cellular life forms, are extremely basic in construction. Whereas cells contain myriad structures that carry out tasks such as respiration and photosynthesis, viruses are basically a packaged set of genes.

Living or not, the ability of viruses to wreak havoc should not be underestimated. The worst outbreak of infectious disease on record occurred in 1918 and 1919, when "Spanish" flu took at least 20 million lives—more than the total killed in the First World War.

Viral epidemics can have far-reaching economic implications, too. Take the outbreak of foot and mouth disease that recently swept through British livestock. The epidemic has cost farmers, the tourist trade, and taxpayers billions of pounds. And viruses that target plants can lay waste to entire crops, destroying farmers' livelihoods. But viruses can also be put to good use in biotechnology. They act as vectors in gene therapy, for example. Some scientists are even attempting to use them to destroy cancerous tissue and to attack antibiotic-resistant bacteria.

Viral genetic material contains all the necessary data, encoded in genes, to replicate and make new virus particles. Unlike cellular life forms, most viruses encode their genetic data as RNA rather than DNA and often in just a single strand. Their genomes are either linear or circular and can exist as one molecule or several segments. RNA viruses are much more fragile than DNA viruses, which limits their size, and have different methods of replicating inside cells.

The Bare Necessities

Compared with other organisms, viruses have relatively few genes. Human cells are estimated to have around 30,000 genes and the *Escherichia coli* bacterium has 4000. Smallpox, a highly contagious virus that caused high fever and a disfiguring rash before it was eradicated in 1977, is one of the largest viruses, containing about 200 genes. At the other end of the range, tiny viruses such as Ebola, HIV, and the measles virus have fewer than 10 genes each.

Each piece of viral genetic material is encased in a protein shell known as a capsid, which is constructed from many spherical capsomeres. The capsid protects the genome from damage and helps the virus to break into host cells. Capsids are generally helical or icosahedral (they are a regular, 20-sided polyhedron). However, some are more complex. Bacteriophages or phages, which target bacteria, have elaborate capsids that consist of a polyhedral "head," in which DNA is stored, and a rod-like "tail." The tail attaches to the bacterium and injects DNA into its cytoplasm. Together, the viral nucleic acid and capsid are called the nucleocapsid.

In some viruses, the whole nucleocapsid is enclosed in a membrane acquired from the host cell and is studded with viral proteins. The viral membrane protein virologists know most about is the spike-shaped haemagglutinin (HA) of influenza. This contains a receptor-binding site, which during infection latches onto specific receptors on the surface of cells lining the nose and lungs. The acidic environment of the nose makes HA contort, thrusting the binding site into a more exposed position on the protein's surface. As a result, the flu virus becomes much more infectious after it has been inhaled.

Like influenza and its HA spike, all viruses use a cell receptor protein to identify and lock onto their particular prey. The cell usually has its own uses for these surface receptors. But the specificity of this "lock-and-key" fit between receptor and receptor-binding protein explains why each type of virus can only infect and replicate in a limited range of host cells. Rabies, for example, is best at invading brain and nervous tissue cells, though different strains can infect a number of mammalian species including dogs, bats, and humans.

Other viruses are so specific that they can only infect a single species—some phages, for example, are only able to colonise *E. coli*.

Once the virus has attached to a receptor, it can penetrate the cell. This is accomplished in various ways. Some viruses take advantage of the cell's own mechanism for importing material, known as receptor-mediated endocytosis. Others, such as the mumps virus, inject their genome into the cell.

In the cytoplasm, the virus discards its protein shell or uncoats—if it has not already left it on the surface. The virus then effectively hijacks the cell's machinery. All living cells constantly retrieve and translate the genetic instructions in their genes. DNA, the stuff of genes, contains the blueprints for making proteins encoded in the "genetic code." Three consecutive bases—a codon—code for an amino acid, a single building block of protein. Each DNA molecule consists of two strands wound together in a double helix.

To make proteins, nuclear DNA is "transcribed" to create a molecule of messenger RNA (mRNA), using the enzyme RNA polymerase. The mRNA then enters the cytoplasm where it acts as a template for synthesising a protein, in a process called "translation." Special cellular structures called ribosomes perform the translation.

Viruses are very effective at taking over these processes to replicate their genomes and produce structural proteins and enzymes. To help themselves on the way, some viruses, such as the poliovirus, produce proteins that enhance viral gene expression and repress cellular gene expression. A process called splicing, in which a single gene can produce a number of different proteins, can also give some viruses an edge over their hosts. Additionally, some viruses can boost the number of different proteins they produce by having overlapping codons, giving different "reading frames," each coding for a different set of proteins. If the start point of transcription is shifted along by a single nucleotide, the virus can produce a different sequence of amino acids. Approximately half of the circular DNA genome of the hepatitis B virus—which attacks liver cells causing nausea, vomiting and intense gut pain—produces proteins from multiple reading frames.

Viruses have different strategies for subjugating cells, depending on the type of genome the virus possesses. In order to form viral mRNAs for making proteins, DNA viruses usually need to gain access to the cell nucleus. There, they use the cell's RNA polymerase to make mRNA molecules. Poxviruses are one of the few DNA viruses that needn't bother getting into the nucleus because they already possess their own copy of the enzyme, enabling them to make an mRNA strand as soon as they get into the cytoplasm. There, the viral mRNAs are transcribed into structural proteins and enzymes using cellular ribosomes. Meanwhile, copies of viral DNA are cranked out at a fast pace in the nucleus, as if it were the cell's own genetic material.

Coded Instructions

There are three kinds of RNA virus: negative-sense viruses, positive-sense viruses, and retroviruses. Rather like photographic film, a negative-sense RNA virus, such as rabies, must first make "complementary" copies of its genetic material in order to translate it into proteins. In the case of positive-sense RNA viruses, the "image" is already the right way round and can be used directly to make proteins. In some cases, viral DNA can be ambisense and possess positive and negative-sense portions.

The third group of RNA viruses, the retroviruses, have a more complex strategy for producing viral mRNAs, in which a copy of the viral genome is integrated into the host cell's DNA. As soon as the retrovirus has infected a cell, a complementary, DNA copy of its RNA genome is produced using the enzyme reverse transcriptase, resulting in an RNA-DNA hybrid. The RNA strand is then digested away from the hybrid by enzymes and replaced by a DNA copy, forming a double-stranded DNA. This is integrated into the cell's own DNA, and is now called proviral DNA. It is transcribed into mRNA in more or less the same way cellular DNA is transcribed. HIV and human T-cell leukaemia virus type 1 (HTLV-1), which causes leukaemia in adults, are examples of retroviruses.

Whatever the type of genome, within a few hours of entering a cell, a virus is capable of manufacturing a million new virus particles with the aid of the cell's raw materials and machinery. The viruses then vacate the pillaged cell in order to find new prey. Some, such as polio, get out by splitting the cell open and are often called bursters. Others, such as influenza and measles, exit by "budding": the virus moves to the edge of the cytoplasm and envelopes itself in the cell's membrane until a section of membrane is able to pinch off completely. In another route of departure, viruses cause neighbouring cells to stick together into complexes called syncytia. The viruses can then move from cell to cell through special protein pores. Such viruses are aptly known as creepers and include the herpes virus.

Cells are usually killed when viruses break out of them, leaving the hallmarks of disease on tissues. Those unsightly red coldsores are the visible result of tissue damage due to the herpes virus. Viruses can also cause damage when large amounts of capsid protein or virus particles build up in cells, inhibiting normal cellular activity and leading to cell death. The nature of the disease caused also depends on the type of cell the virus targets. Rabies, for instance, infects brain cells and therefore causes symptoms such as dementia and extreme thirst. HIV, which singles out immune cells, reduces the body's natural immunity and makes it vulnerable to opportunistic infections such as tuberculosis and virus-induced cancers. Alternatively, damage may be inflicted when the body's defences kill off infected cells, causing the rash seen in measles, for example.

Some viruses act at their point of entry into the body. Adenoviruses, for example, invades cells of the conjunctiva in the eye and cause conjunctivitis, in which the eyes become red, itchy, and sore. Such viruses generally cause acute symptoms soon after infection that last a few hours to a week. Some, however, move beyond the point of entry and spread around the body, producing a generalised infection in many tissues, including lymph nodes, liver, and bone marrow, before settling in a specific tissue. Generalised infections are poorly understood, but have longer incubation times—the time lag between infection and the appearance of symptoms. Examples include measles virus, varicella (which causes chickenpox), and mumps.

Other viral diseases only rear their ugly heads a few years after infection, or else at intervals. Hepatitis B is one of many such infections. Sufferers may experience bouts of fever and pain every few years when the virus starts to actively replicate. Such a situation can occur when the viral DNA persists in the host cell. This can either be as proviral DNA integrated into a chromosome in the case of retroviruses, or in a separate, circular DNA molecule called an episome. Sometimes proviral DNA can upset cell functioning to such a degree that the cell becomes cancerous.

Whatever the disease caused, viruses eventually leave the body and are transmitted to other hosts. A virus may be coughed or sneezed out of the lungs and inhaled by another host, for example. Or it may be transmitted sexually or via a "faecal-oral" route, in which traces of infected faeces are swallowed and assimilated through the gut. Faecal-oral transmission is common where sanitation is poor. In addition, viruses can enter new hosts via blood transfusion, surgery, and organ transplantation.

One of the most disquieting things about viruses is their apparent ability to spring up out of nowhere and re-emerge after many years. Even more disturbing, many viruses are able to evade attempts to control them using vaccines and drugs. Over the past few decades, humans have been subjected to an increasing number of viral assaults for which we have no cure. These include HIV, which now infects more than 100,000 people every week, and the horrific outbreaks of haemorrhagic fevers in parts of Africa, such as Ebola, which cause sufferers to bleed internally, collapse, and die. Then there was the outbreak of a lethal strain of flu in Hong Kong in 1997.

So how do new viruses surface? The evolution of existing pathogens into different, more deadly forms is a key source of novel viral disease. Changes in a virus's DNA or RNA can modify aspects of its behaviour, such as its virulence or the range of species and tissues it can infect.

Creating a Monster

Viral genetic evolution occurs through two main mechanisms. First, different viruses can swap genes, or part of their genes. This process of recombination is common in viruses whose genomes are made up of discrete segments—in these cases, the process is also called reassortment. The 1997 outbreak of "bird" flu in Hong Kong occurred when a strain of avian influenza in chickens exchanged an entire genetic segment with a human flu virus, enabling it to infect people. In RNA viruses without segmented genomes, recombination is thought to occur when the RNA polymerase enzyme switches to the equivalent gene on another virus during replication.

The second fuel powering the evolution of RNA viruses is point mutation, in which a single nucleotide is altered. The mutation rate is much faster in viruses than humans, because viruses replicate rapidly and have less efficient DNA repair systems. But the rate of change is even speedier in RNA viruses than DNA viruses, because RNA enzymes are not backed up by a cellular editing or proof-reading system (unlike DNA polymerase). As a result, there's a huge amount of genetic variability within a new generation of RNA viruses, although many will be defective. This explains why HIV can quickly become resistant to new drugs. Strange as it may sound, versions of HIV that are resistant to drugs that have yet to be invented may already exist. Similarly, flu can strike down the same victim every year because the virus can evolve into a form the immune system cannot recognise.

New viruses often emerge when people come into increased contact with other hosts (animal, plant, or human). This may have taken place with increased frequency between 8000 and 10,000 years ago when humans first began to domesticate animals and live in large sedentary groups. As a result of our daily proximity with animals, pathogens were easily able to evolve into forms that could infect humans. Both smallpox and measles viruses evolved from cattle viruses, while flu probably originated in ducks or pigs. Today, population pressure often causes humans to colonise new areas, such as forests, increasing the risk of new viral disease.

An increase in the size of the animal host population harbouring the virus can also shift the balance and trigger disease in humans. The lethal Sin Nombre virus, which targets the lungs, swept through the mid-southwest US in

1993 when the local deer mouse population shot up. As a result, people increasingly came into contact with infected mouse faeces and urine.

Changing human and environmental factors can transform an isolated disease into a worldwide epidemic (pandemic). HIV is perhaps the ultimate example. Thought to have originated from contact with African apes and monkeys, HIV reached epidemic proportions in the 1980s as a result of technological and social factors, including blood transfusion technology, international travel, sexual promiscuity, and intravenous drug abuse.

New molecular technologies that have improved our ability to recognise and classify viruses also give the impression that viruses are running wild. Take the hepatitis viruses, which all infect liver cells. Around 15 years ago only hepatitis A and B were known; now viruses C, D, E, and G have also been isolated.

So although at first glance it may seem as if new viruses are appearing out of nowhere, they are not. They are either evolving from existing bugs, have been given a new chance to spread, or have merely been recognised for the first time. Nevertheless, researchers now face a considerable challenge in beating viral diseases. What's more, many believe that illnesses ranging from diabetes to obesity and Gulf War syndrome could be triggered by viruses. Fortunately, our understanding of virus life cycles and genetics is growing. For instance, HIV's high mutation rate could well prove to be its Achilles' heel. Drug designers think that by artificially increasing its mutation rate they could transform new generations of the virus into defective mutants unable to infect cells.

There are other more practical benefits, too. The rapid and efficient response to the 1995 Ebola outbreak in Kitwit, Zaire (now the Democratic Republic of Congo) was made possible thanks to DNA technology. Samples were flown to the Centers for Disease Control and Prevention in Atlanta and within two days a capsid protein gene had been sequenced, and the agent was identified. As a result, appropriate measures could be taken to curb the spread of the disease.

We may have lost many battles to viruses, but the war is far from over. We are learning how to outwit one of humankind's deadliest enemies.

In the Beginning Was the Virus

As viruses do not leave fossils, deducing their origins is a tricky business. Many biologists believe that, because they are totally dependent on living cells to replicate, they originated in cells. Also, many viral genes have uncanny similarities to cellular genes. In fact, viral genes tend to have more in common with cellular genes than with each other.

According to this theory, the likeliest viral ancestors were mobile cellular genetic elements, such as transposons and plasmids. Transposons are small segments of DNA that jump from one place to another in cell genomes, whereas plasmids are small circular DNAs, separate from chromosomes, that inhabit yeast and bacteria. Like viruses, plasmids can move between cells.

Another theory is based on the logic that simple life forms usually precede more complex ones. It proposes that viruses are descendants of free-living self-replicating RNA and DNA molecules, which also evolved into cellular life some three billion years ago. A number of lines of evidence support this view. First, ribozymes, RNA molecules that act like enzymes to speed up some cellular reactions, can self-replicate, suggesting that similar sorts of molecule could be the ancestors of RNA viruses. In addition, there is evidence that some viruses are ancient and lived inside their hosts even before the latter evolved into the species we see today.

It's possible both theories have some truth and that viruses have been created throughout the history of life.

Seeing the Wood for the Trees

All organisms gradually accumulate mutations in their DNA over time. Therefore, species that are more closely related to each other usually differ by fewer mutations than more distantly related species. As a result, contemporary DNA sequences contain a record of evolutionary history. The same is true for viruses, and the information can be used to construct viral family trees, otherwise known as phylogenies.

Constructing phylogenies allows us to understand how new infections appear and propagate. Viruses spread through different populations at different times and by different routes. Therefore, branches may be clustered according to geography, virulence, host type, or time. For example, hepatitis B virus, one of the most infectious human diseases, has six clusters worldwide (labelled A to

F). A is common in northern and central Europe, while B and C are prevalent in Asia. D and E are common in the Mediterranean region and Africa respectively, and F exists in the Americas. What's more, further subdivisions or branches can separate viruses by how well they respond to treatment or by the syndrome they produce in their host. For hepatitis B virus, for example, some branches denote dangerous "killer" strains, while others are less harmful. In fact, DNA analysis is powerful enough to identify the particular nucleotide in a gene that can change a mediocre virus into a serial killer—which could be invaluable in designing drugs and vaccines.

Looking at the proportions of branches on a tree can give an insight into the history of an epidemic. Take HIV-1, which is broadly divided into nine main lineages or subtypes. Subtype A, found in parts of Africa, has been spread predominantly by heterosexual intercourse. It has many branches, which harbour a great deal of genetic diversity, indicating that it has existed in the host population for a long time. In contrast, subtype B, resident in Europe and the US, is associated with the HIV epidemic in homosexual men and drug users. Subtype B has much less genetic diversity than subtype A, and forms tighter clusters of branches, implying a more recent emergence.

Reprinted with permission from *New Scientist*.

Viral entry into animal cells is a complex process of stealth and trickery. First, the virus

must bind to the host cell in a way that does not reveal an attack. Next, the bound virus must induce the cell to bring it inside its membrane. Once inside the cell, the virus must uncoat its nucleic acid core and import itself into the nucleus, where its genes can be transcribed. Along the way, the virus must avoid triggering the cell's suicide mechanism, digestion in the lysosome, entrapment in the cytoplasm, or a failure to enter into the nucleus. In this article, two researchers from the Swiss Federal Institute of Technology–Zurich, Dr. Ari Helenius, a professor, and Dr. Alicia Smith, a postdoctoral fellow, explain how different classes of virus approach each of these steps. By gaining a clear understanding of each step in detail, they argue, biologists are likely to be able to design more effective antiviral drugs. —JL

From "How Viruses Enter Animal Cells"
by Alicia E. Smith and Ari Helenius
Science, **April 9, 2004**

Viruses replicate within living cells and use the cellular machinery for the synthesis of their genome and other components. To gain access, they have evolved a variety of elegant mechanisms to deliver their genes and accessory proteins into the host cell. Many animal viruses take advantage of endocytic pathways and rely on the cell to guide them through a complex entry and uncoating program. In the dialogue between the cell and the intruder, the cell provides critical cues that allow the virus to undergo molecular transformations that lead to successful internalization, intra-cellular transport, and uncoating.

Although extremely simple in structure and composition, viruses are masters of camouflage and deception. Devoid of any means of independent locomotion, they disseminate by exploiting cells and organisms. Aided by rodents, insects, and migratory birds, and passed along by global trade and travel, they move around the world with amazing speed. Once they enter the body of a potential host, they can penetrate mucus layers, move through the blood stream, and disperse with the help of motile cells and neuronal pathways.

A critical moment occurs when a virus particle reaches a potential host cell and attaches itself to the surface. It must now deliver its capsid and accessory proteins into the cell in a replication-competent form, ideally with minimal damage to the cell and leaving little evidence of its entry for detection by the immune defenses. This is not a trivial problem because cell membranes are impermeable to macromolecules.

Overview: Virus Entry and Uncoating

Viral particles mediate the transfer of the viral genome and accessory proteins from an infected host cell to a noninfected host cell. The task involves packaging the viral genome (RNA or DNA) and accessory proteins, releasing the package from the infected cell, protecting the essential components during extracellular transmission, and delivering them into a new host cell. Many viruses with a DNA genome must enter the nucleus, whereas RNA viruses, with a few exceptions, replicate in the cytosol. Overall, viruses use a "Trojan horse" strategy in which the victim assists the intruder. To extract assistance from the host cell, viruses use the detailed "insider information" that they have acquired during millions of years of coevolution with their hosts.

In a typical animal virus particle, the viral RNA or DNA is condensed in icosahedral or helical nucleoprotein complexes called capsids. In enveloped viruses, the capsids are surrounded by a lipid bilayer that contains viral spike glycoproteins. In addition, some viruses contain reverse transcriptases, RNA polymerases, kinases, and other proteins that are important during uncoating, replication, or other early intracellular steps.

To infect a target cell, a virus particle proceeds through a multistep entry process, during which each step is preprogrammed and tightly regulated in time and space: virus binding to the cell, endocytosis, and nuclear import. Another critical step in the infection process is uncoating, during which the lipid envelope must be shed and the capsids must be at least partially disassembled to expose a replication-competent genome. Once uncoating has occurred, the mobility of the genome within the cell is restricted.

Progress through the entry and uncoating program depends on "cues" that the cell provides. Cues include interaction with cell surface receptors, exposure to low pH, and reimmersion into a reducing environment. Such cues trigger preprogrammed conformational changes and dissociation events in the virus particle.

To respond to cues, the virus particles or some of their component proteins (such as the spike glycoproteins) occur in metastable and easily modified conformational states. When triggered by a cue, the metastable state can be relaxed to allow marked changes in viral properties without the input of external energy. Here, we describe several examples of this process.

Receptors and Attachment Factors

To infect, a virus must first attach itself to the surface of a cell. The molecules to which viruses bind constitute a diverse collection of cellular proteins, carbohydrates, and lipids. They differ from one virus to the next, and they range from abundant and ubiquitous to rare and cell specific. Some of them merely serve as attachment factors that concentrate viruses on the cell's surface. Others are true receptors in that they not only bind viruses but are also responsible for guiding the bound viruses into endocytic pathways and for transmitting signals to the cytoplasm. Receptors can also serve as cues that induce conformational changes that lead to membrane fusion and penetration. The identity and distribution of attachment factors and receptors determines to a large extent which cell types, tissues, and organisms a virus can infect . . .

Receptor-Binding Proteins

In enveloped viruses, it is the spike glycoproteins that bind to receptors. They are often multifunctional proteins serving additionally as membrane fusion factors and/or receptor-destroying enzymes . . .

. . . In non-enveloped viruses, the structures that bind receptors are projections or indentations in the capsid surface. In rhino- and enteroviruses, including polio, the receptors bind in a cleft in the capsid surface called the "canyon."[16] For some viruses, binding may cause destabilization of the virus particle, a first step toward uncoating.

Virus Binding: Carbohydrate/Protein Interactions

Carbohydrate/protein interactions have long been known to play an important role in viral invasion.[17] Some viruses bind specifically to sialic acid–containing groups, and others bind to glycosaminoglycans or glycolipids. Heparan sulfate has been identified as an attachment factor for herpes viruses, adeno-associated viruses, dengue virus, tick-borne encephalitis virus, papilloma viruses, paramyxovirus 3, and Sindbis virus . . .[6, 18–23]

. . . In most cases, carbohydrates serve as attachment factors that do not trigger conformational changes . . .

. . . In some virus systems, the lectin is located on the cell surface and the carbohydrate ligand is located on the virus. HIV-1, Sindbis virus, Dengue virus, human cytomegalovirus, hepatitis C virus, and Ebola virus all bind to cell surface lectins . . .[27–32]

Endocytosis

Many animal viruses rely on the cell's endocytic machinery for productive infection . . . One of the advantages of endocytic entry is that viruses are given a "free ride" deep into the cytoplasm. This is because endocytic vesicles are designed to traverse the barriers imposed by the cortical cytoskeleton and the highly structured cytoplasm. Depending on the virus, incoming virus particles can be seen entering endosomal structures, lysosomes, the endoplasmic reticulum (ER), and occasionally the Golgi complex.[33, 34]

A further advantage of endocytosis is that incoming viruses are exposed to compartmental environments that differ from the extracellular milieu. For many viruses, the mildly acidic pH in endosomes provides an essential cue that triggers penetration and uncoating.[35-37] Penetration from intracellular vacuoles also has the advantage of leaving no viral glycoproteins exposed on the cell surface for immune detection. Finally, if penetration is lytic—as is the case for adenoviruses— endosomal membrane lysis is likely to be less damaging to the cell than lysis of the plasma membrane.

One risk during endocytosis is possible delivery to the lysosome, a degradative compartment and a dead-end for most viruses. This is why viruses have carefully adjusted the threshold pH for activation to match that of early (pH 6 to 6.5) or late endosomes (pH 5 to 6).[38, 39]

. . . The progress of individual virus particles through endocytic compartments can be tracked with real-time video microscopy.[41-44] Individual fluorescent virus particles can be observed to bind to the cell surface, diffuse along the membrane, get trapped in coated pits or caveolae, enter by endocytosis, move along microtubules, and so on. With the use of specific fluorescent dyes, the acidification of virus particles and the fusion of the viral envelope with cellular membranes can be monitored.

Lipid Raft–Mediated Endocytosis of Viruses

SV40 and some other viruses choose endocytic pathways that bypass clathrin-mediated endocytosis. One of these involves caveolae, flask-shaped indentations of the plasma membrane enriched in cholesterol and sphingolipids, caveolins, and signaling factors.[45-48] Although generally immobile, caveolae are known to support the internalization of certain physiological ligands . . .[49-51]

In addition to the caveolae, it is evident that cells have other clathrin-independent pathways of endocytosis.[55, 61] These noncaveolar, lipid raft–dependent pathways are still poorly characterized. They may serve as a primary entry route for viruses such as polyoma[59, 62] and as an alternative entry route for SV40 in cells that lack caveolae.[63]

The presence of multiple pathways and previously unobserved endocytic organelles challenges established assumptions about the entry of many viruses. Cellular processes can be more complex than anticipated, which is illustrated by the recent observation that influenza virus, which was thought to enter by clathrin-coated pit endocytosis, can infect cells in which clathrin-coated vesicle transport is blocked.[64]

Penetration

Penetration of enveloped viruses occurs by membrane fusion catalyzed by fusion proteins in the viral envelope. The machinery involved is rather simple, at least when compared to the apparatus needed for intracellular membrane-fusion events. One reason for simplicity is that viral fusion factors are used only once. Fusion activity is triggered by cues in the form of receptor binding or low pH (as mentioned above). They induce, as a rule, irreversible conformational changes . . .

Membrane fusion is an elegant and effective way to deliver viral capsids into the cytosol. No macromolecular assemblies need to pass through a hydrophobic membrane barrier. The underlying principle is the same as in intracellular membrane traffic; the viral envelope is a "transport vesicle," and the capsid is the cargo.

Because nonenveloped viruses do not have a membrane, they penetrate either by lysing a membrane or by creating a porelike structure in a membrane. Although details remain obscure, it is clear that penetration of non-enveloped viruses also involves cooperative changes in virus particles triggered by receptor binding or low pH.[16, 72, 73] The viruses become more hydrophobic and interact with membranes directly . . .

Intracellular Transport

After penetration, the genome of most viruses must be transported either to the nucleus or to specific cytosolic membranes. Diffusion in the crowded and highly structured cytosol is not efficient given the large dimensions of most capsids and the long distances they must travel.[77, 78] To move inside the cell, incoming viruses often exploit the cytoskeleton and cellular motor proteins. As recently reviewed,[77] there are two main ways to do this; the viruses can allow endocytic vesicles to ferry them as passive lumenal cargo, or the penetrated capsid can itself interact with the relevant motors. In the latter case, a capsid protein binds and interacts with the cellular factors . . .

Signaling During Virus Entry

In recent years, it has become clear that the information exchange between incoming viruses and the host cell is not limited to cues given to the virus by the cell. For many viruses, it takes the form of a two-way dialogue in which the virus takes advantage of the cell's own signal transduction systems to transmit signals to the cell.[82, 83] These signals induce changes that facilitate entry, prepare the cell for invasion, and neutralize host defenses.

The signals are usually generated at the cell surface through the virus binding to receptors that are themselves signaling molecules or modulators (e.g., growth factor receptors, chemokine receptors, integrins, and gangliosides) and can be activated by virus binding or virus-induced clustering . . . Human cytomegalovirus, a herpes virus, activates several signaling pathways through the interaction between envelope glycoprotein B and the epidermal growth-factor receptor.[85]

Nuclear Import

The nucleus provides excellent "service" functions for virus replication, ranging from DNA and RNA polymerases to RNA-splicing and -modifying enzymes. However, the nucleus is difficult to enter and exit, and viruses must again rely on cellular mechanisms.[56, 86, 87]

In interphase cells, the import of virus and viral capsids occurs through the NPCs. For targeting, viruses use nuclear localization signals and cytosolic import receptors.

Recent studies show that the upper limit in particle diameter for transport through the NPC is 39 nm.[93] The smallest viruses and capsids, as well as helical capsids in extended form, can therefore be imported into the nucleus without disassembly or deformation. Among icosahedral particles, parvoviruses (diameter 18 to 24 nm) and the capsids of hepatitis B virus (diameter 36 nm) are probably imported intact.[94] The capsids of hepatitis B virus are uncoated in the basket on the nuclear side of the pore complex.[95]

Larger viruses and capsids must either be deformed or disassemble to allow the genome to pass through the NPC . . .

With the exception of lentiviruses such as HIV-1, retroviruses do not use the NPCs for nuclear entry. Preintegration complexes can only enter the nucleus during mitosis when the nuclear envelope is temporarily absent, limiting their infectivity to dividing cells.

Direct Cell-to-Cell Transfer With and Without Virus Infection

Finally, infection can be transmitted directly from cell to cell. Viruses such as measles, which express in the plasma membrane envelope proteins that are fusogenic at neutral pH, often induce fusion of infected cells with uninfected neighboring cells. Thus, the viral genes pass directly from cell to cell, and infection occurs without the involvement of viral particles.

In an alternative strategy for cell-to-cell transfer, extra-cellular vaccinia virus particles are practically pushed into an adjacent cell by localized actin polymerization on the inside of the infected cell.[101] The polymerization of actin is triggered by a viral protein that recruits the plasma membrane . . .

The observation that HIV-1 and other lentiviruses in some cell types bud into endosome-like vacuoles has raised the possibility that virus particles can be released by the infected cell in a polarized fashion by means of regulated secretion.[102] HIV-1 particles may, in this case, be directly transmitted from a macrophage to a T cell as part of the normal cell-to-cell interaction. There is also evidence that dendritic cells, without getting infected, may concentrate HIV-1 in regions of cell-to-cell contact and thus promote infection.[103, 104]

Perspectives

Viruses continue to pose a serious threat to the life and well-being of humans, animals, and other organisms. In the past, the search for antiviral drugs was focused mainly on replicases and other viral enzymes. That entry and uncoating can serve as a target for antivirals has recently been demonstrated by new inhibitors against influenza neuraminidase and the fusion protein of HIV-1.[105, 106] With our information rapidly reaching the molecular level, it may be possible to develop new approaches to block the entry of viruses . . .[107]

Careful analysis of early virus-cell interactions is [also] likely to extend our still incomplete understanding of plasma membrane dynamics, membrane fusion, endocytic pathways, and many other aspects of cell function.

End Notes

1. S. Pohlmann, F. Baribaud, R. W. Doms, *Trends Immunol.* 22, 643 (2001).

2. A. A. Bashirova *et al.*, *J. Exp. Med.* 193, 671 (2001).

3. Y. Feng, C. C. Broder, P. E. Kennedy, E. A. Berger, *Science* 272, 872 (1996).

4. C. M. Carr, P. S. Kim, *Cell* 73, 823 (1993).

5. S. A. Gallo *et al.*, *Biochim. Biophys. Acta* 1614, 36 (2003).

6. P. G. Spear, R. J. Eisenberg, G. H. Cohen, *Virology* 275, 1 (2000).

7. J. J. Skehel, D. C. Wiley, *Annu. Rev. Biochem.* 69, 531 (2000).

8. T. Stehle, Y. Yan, T. L. Benjamin, S. C. Harrison, *Nature* 369, 160 (1994).

9. P. M. Colman, C. W. Ward, *Curr. Top. Microbiol. Immunol.* 114, 177 (1985).

10. P. D. Kwong *et al.*, *Nature* 393, 648 (1998).

11. A. Carfi *et al.*, *Mol. Cell* 8, 169 (2001).

12. M. M. Mullen, K. M. Haan, R. Longnecker, T. S. Jardetzky, *Mol. Cell* 9, 375 (2002).

13. S. Crennell, T. Takimoto, A. Portner, G. Taylor, *Nature Struct. Biol.* 7, 1068 (2000).

14. M. C. Bewley, K. Springer, Y. B. Zhang, P. Freimuth, J. M. Flanagan, *Science* 286, 1579 (1999).

15. P. L. Stewart, T. S. Dermody, G. R. Nemerow, *Adv. Protein Chem.* 64, 455 (2003).

16. M. G. Rossmann, Y. He, R. J. Kuhn, *Trends Microbiol.* 10, 324 (2002).

17. K. Lonberg-Holm, L. Philipson, *Monogr. Virol.* 9, 1 (1974).

18. A. P. Byrnes, D. E. Griffin, *J. Virol.* 72, 7349 (1998).

19. C. Summerford, R. J. Samulski, *J. Virol.* 72, 1438 (1998).

20. Y. Chen *et al.*, *Nature Med.* 3, 866 (1997).

21. H. Kroschewski, S. L. Allison, F. X. Heinz, C. W. Mandl, *Virology* 308, 92 (2003).

22. P. Drobni, N. Mistry, N. McMillan, M. Evander, *Virology* 310, 163 (2003).

23. S. Bose, A. K. Banerjee, *Virology* 298, 73 (2002).

24. E. Trybala *et al.*, *Virology* 218, 35 (1996).

25. B. Tsai *et al.*, *EMBO J.* 22, 4346 (2003).

26. A. E. Smith, H. Lilie, A. Helenius, *FEBS Lett.* 555, 199 (2003).

27. F. Halary *et al.*, *Immunity* 17, 653 (2002).

28. H. Feinberg, D. A. Mitchell, K. Drickamer, W. I. Weis, *Science* 294, 2163 (2001).

29. S. Pohlmann *et al.*, *J. Virol.* 77, 4070 (2003).

30. G. Simmons *et al.*, *Virology* 305, 115 (2003).

31. P. Y. Lozach *et al.*, *J. Biol. Chem.* 278, 20358 (2003).

32. B. Tassaneetrithep *et al.*, *J. Exp. Med.* 197, 823 (2003).

33. S. Dales, *Bacteriol. Rev.* 37, 103 (1973).

34. U. Bantel-Schaal, B. Hub, J. Kartenbeck, *J. Virol.* 76, 2340 (2002).

35. A. Helenius, J. Kartenbeck, K. Simons, E. Fries, *J. Cell Biol.* 84 ,404 (1980).

36. M. Marsh, A. Helenius, *Adv. Virus Res.* 36, 107 (1989).

37. K. Martin, A. Helenius, *Cell* 67, 117 (1991).

38. M. Kielian, M. Marsh, A. Helenius, *J. Cell Biol.* 101, 1086a (1985).

39. S. Schmid, R. Fuchs, M. Kielian, A. Helenius, I. Mellman, *J. Cell Biol.* 108, 1291 (1989).

40. S. B. Sieczkarski, G. R. Whittaker, *Traffic* 4, 333 (2003).

41. M. Suomalainen *et al., J. Cell Biol.* 144, 657 (1999).

42. L. Pelkmans, J. Kartenbeck, A. Helenius, *Nature Cell Biol.* 3, 473 (2001).

43. G. Seisenberger *et al., Science* 294, 1929 (2001).

44. M. Lakadamyali, M. J. Rust, H. P. Babcock, X. Zhuang, *Proc. Natl. Acad. Sci. U.S.A.* 100, 9280 (2003).

45. R. G. Parton, *Curr. Opin. Cell Biol.* 8, 542 (1996).

46. B. Razani, S. E. Woodman, M. P. Lisanti, *Pharmacol. Rev.* 54, 431 (2002).

47. R. G. Anderson, *Annu. Rev. Biochem.* 67, 199 (1998).

48. P. Thomsen, K. Roepstorff, M. Stahlhut, B. van Deurs, *Mol. Biol. Cell* 13, 238 (2002).

49. B. J. Nichols, *Nature Cell Biol.* 4, 374 (2002).

50. P. U. Le, I. R. Nabi, *J. Cell Sci.* 116, 1059 (2003).

51. I. R. Nabi, P. U. Le, *J. Cell Biol.* 161, 673 (2003).

52. L. Pelkmans, D. Puntener, A. Helenius, *Science* 296, 535 (2002).

53. L. C. Norkin, *Adv. Drug Deliv. Rev.* 49, 301 (2001).

54. R. G. Parton, A. A. Richards, *Traffic* 4, 724 (2003).

55. L. Pelkmans, A. Helenius, *Curr. Opin. Cell Biol.* 15, 414 (2003).

56. H. Kasamatsu, A. Nakanishi, *Annu. Rev. Microbiol.* 52, 627 (1998).

57. V. Marjomaki *et al., J. Virol.* 76, 1856 (2002).

58. Z. Richterova *et al., J. Virol.* 75, 10880 (2001).

59. J. M. Gilbert, I. G. Goldberg, T. L. Benjamin, *J. Virol.* 77, 2615 (2003).

60. L. Bousarghin, A. Touze, P. Y. Sizaret, P. Coursaget, *J. Virol.* 77, 3846 (2003).

61. S. D. Conner, S. L. Schmid, *Nature* 422, 37 (2003).

62. A. E. Smith, H. Ewers, R. Mancini, H. Lilie, A. Helenius, unpublished data.

63. E. M. Damm, L. Pelkmans, T. Kurzhalia, A. Helenius, unpublished data.

64. S. B. Sieczkarski, G. R. Whittaker, *J. Virol.* 76, 10455 (2002).

65. M. Kielian, *Adv. Virus Res.* 45, 113 (1995).

66. P. M. Colman, M. C. Lawrence, *Nature Rev. Mol. Cell Biol.* 4, 309 (2003).

67. W. Weissenhorn *et al., Mol. Membr. Biol.* 16, 3 (1999).

68. F. X. Heinz, S. L. Allison, *Curr. Opin. Microbiol.* 4, 450 (2001).

69. D. L. Gibbons *et al., Cell* 114, 573 (2003).

70. D. L. Gibbons *et al., Nature* 427, 320 (2004).

71. Y. Modis S. Ogata, D. Clements, S. C. Harrison, *Nature* 427, 313 (2004).

72. J. M. Hogle, *Annu. Rev. Microbiol.* 56, 677 (2002).

73. M. M. Poranen, R. Daugelavicius, D. H. Bamford, *Annu. Rev. Microbiol.* 56, 521 (2002).

74. D. J. P. Fitzgerald, R. Padmanabhan, I. Pastan, M. C. Willigham, *Cell* 32, 607 (1983).

75. R. Blumenthal, P. Seth, M. C. Willingham, I. Pastan, *Biochemistry* 25, 2231 (1986).

76. K. Chandran, D. L. Farsetta, M. L. Nibert, *J. Virol.* 76, 9920 (2002).

77. B. Sodeik, *Trends Microbiol.* 8, 465 (2000).

78. M. J. Tomishima, G. A. Smith, L. W. Enquist, *Traffic* 2, 429 (2001).

79. M. Marsh, R. Bron, *J. Cell Sci.* 110, 95 (1997).

80. L. M. Lanier, J. M. Slack, L. E. Volkman, *Virology* 216, 380 (1996).

81. L. M. Machesky, R. H. Insall, L. E. Volkman, *Trends Cell Biol.* 11, 286 (2001).

82. G. R. Nemerow, *Virology* 274, 1 (2000).

83. U. F. Greber, *Cell. Mol. Life Sci.* 59, 608 (2002).

84. L. K. Medina-Kauwe, *Adv. Drug Deliv. Rev.* 55, 1485 (2003).

85. X. Wang, S. M. Huong, M. L. Chiu, N. Raab-Traub, E. S. Huang, *Nature* 424, 456 (2003).

86. G. R. Whittaker, M. Kann, A. Helenius, *Annu. Rev. Cell Dev. Biol.* 16, 627 (2000).

87. G. R. Whittaker, *Adv. Drug Deliv. Rev.* 55, 733 (2003).

88. E. Merle, R. C. Rose, L. LeRoux, J. Moroianu, *J. Cell. Biochem.* 74, 628 (1999).

89. L. M. Nelson *et al.*, *J. Cell. Biochem.* 79, 225 (2000).

90. M. Kann, B. Sodeik, A. Vlachou, W. H. Gerlich, A. Helenius, *J. Cell Biol.* 145, 45 (1999).

91. R. E. O 'Neill, R. Jaskunas, G. Blobel, P. Palese, J. Moroianu, *J. Biol. Chem.* 270, 22701 (1995).

92. L. C. Trotman, N. Mosberger, M. Fornerod, R. P. Stidwill, U. F. Greber, *Nature Cell Biol.* 3, 1092 (2001).

93. N. Pante, M. Kann, *Mol. Biol. Cell* 13, 425 (2002).

94. U. F. Greber, A. Fassati, *Traffic* 4, 136 (2003).

95. B. Rabe, A. Vlachou, N. Pante, A. Helenius, M. Kann, *roc. Natl. Acad. Sci. U.S.A.* 100, 9849 (2003).

96. P. M. Ojala, B. Sodeik, M. W. Ebersold, U. Kutay, A. Helenius, *Mol. Cell. Biol.* 20, 4922 (2000).

97. W. W. Newcomb *et al.*, *J. Virol.* 75, 10923 (2001).

98. B. Sodeik, M. W. Ebersold, A. Helenius, *J. Cell Biol.* 136, 1007 (1997).

99. M. P. Sherman, W. C. Greene, *Microbes Infect.* 4, 67 (2002).

100. B. R. Cullen, *Cell* 105, 697 (2001).

101. G. L. Smith, B. J. Murphy, M. Law, *Annu. Rev. Microbiol.* 57, 323 (2003).

102. A. Pelchen-Matthews, B. Kramer, M. Marsh, *J. CellBiol.* 162, 443 (2003).

103. D. S. Kwon, G. Gregorio, N. Bitton, W. A. Hendrickson, D. R. Littman, *Immunity* 16, 135 (2002).

104. D. McDonald *et al.*, *Science* 300 ,1295 (2003).

105. S. K. Sia, P. A. Carr, A. G. Cochran, V. N. Malashkevich, P. S. Kim, *Proc. Natl. Acad. Sci. U.S.A.* 99,14664 (2002).

106. B. J. Smith *et al.*, *J. Med. Chem.* 45, 2207 (2002).

107. T. C. Pierson, R. W. Doms, *Curr. Top. Microbiol. Immunol.* 281,1 (2003).

108. F. Reggiori, H. R. Pelham, Nature Cell Biol. 4 ,117 (2002).

109. L. D. Hernandez, L. R. Hoffman, T. G. Wolfsberg, J. M. White, *Annu. Rev. Cell Dev. Biol.* 12, 627 (1996).

Before concluding that all viruses are dangerous and deadly, remember for a moment that certain viruses—bacteriophages—can infect only bacteria. These viruses have no effect on human cells. Early in the twentieth century, doctors and biologists wondered if bacteriophages could be used to cure bacterial infections in humans. In some early attempts, it did seem to work. When penicillin and other antibiotics were discovered, phage treatments were forgotten in the United States. Currently, antibiotic overuse has contributed to the rise of antibiotic-resistant bacteria, and many common antibiotics are now nearly useless. This article highlights the work of Dr. Alexander Sulakvelidze, a professor at the University of Maryland and the cofounder of a company called Intralytix. Intralytix, along with several other companies, is trying to isolate phages from nature that can specifically kill antibiotic-resistant bacteria such as those that cause tuberculosis. Although it is still in its infancy, this idea could be the key to regaining the upper hand in many bacterial infections. —JL

"The Return of the Phage"
by Julie Wakefield
Smithsonian Magazine, October 2000

Amid the din from street musicians, panhandlers, and baby-toting moms along Baltimore's Inner Harbor, a petite woman wearing surgical gloves squats down on an embankment wall. She dips a sterile white bucket into the water, pulls it up, then peels off her gloves, and in seconds vanishes.

Few onlookers would guess Ekaterine Chighladze is a mercenary in a microscopic war. She marches the unsavory water past Camden Yards, the Baltimore Orioles' playground, and ducks into a lab of the University of Maryland.

She repeats this process every two weeks. So even before her analysis, she knows the bucket is chock-full of naturally occurring predatory viruses called bacterio-phages—phages for short. After more than a half century of neglect in the West, these tiny viruses are gaining new consideration as slayers of so-called super-bugs—those often deadly bacteria ever more resistant to conventional drug treatment.

"Modern medicine could be set back to its pre-antibiotic days," Alexander Sulakvelidze, who runs the lab, says from behind a lab bench piled high with agar dishes of bacteria. In 1998 the professor of medi-cine cofounded a Baltimore company called Intralytix to manufacture phages. "All the advances that we take such pride in, from transplants to chemotherapy," he says, "may become impossible when bacteria develop resistance to antibiotics."

According to a recent World Health Organization (WHO) report, nearly all gonorrhea strains are unchecked by penicillin in Southeast Asia. In India, typhoid species have developed resistance to three drugs commonly used against them. Drug-resistant tuberculosis has invaded one in ten TB patients in Estonia, Latvia, and parts of Russia and China. In Thailand, the top three antimalarial drugs have been rendered useless.

"The phenomenon isn't just happening in developing nations," says Richard Honour, president and CEO of Phage Therapeutics International, a fledgling company in Bothell, Washington. "More American lives are lost each year to antibiotic-resistant bacterial infections than were claimed by the entire Vietnam War," he says. The WHO reports that some 14,000 people die each year just from drug-resistant infections picked up in U.S. hospitals. Worldwide, up to 60 percent of hospital-acquired infections turn out to be drug-resistant.

Phages are among the simplest organisms on the planet. About a millionth of an inch in size, a fraction of most bacteria, phages become visible only under an electron microscope. A milliliter of water can contain up to a trillion. They thrive anywhere bacteria can exist—in raw sewage, open water, humans, and practically everywhere else, says Carl Merril, chief of the biochemical genetics lab at the National Institute of Mental Health (NIMH). Some phages reproduce by invading a bacterium and forcing it to manufacture copies of the phage until the host is overwhelmed, he explains. Eventually, the progeny either dissolve or burst the cell wall, destroying the host bacterium, and move on, ready to prey on surrounding bacteria. A single phage can produce tens of thousands of offspring in an hour, growing exponentially from there. Other phages reproduce by becoming a part of the bacterium's genome. When the bacterium reproduces, so does the phage.

Human phage therapy is hardly new. Before the discovery of penicillin, pioneering doctors around the world employed phages as healers, giving them by potion or injection. These stalkers of bacteria were discovered during World War I by British bacteriologist Frederick Twort and independently two years later by the French-Canadian Felix D'Herelle, a self-taught medical maverick then at the Pasteur Institute in Paris. Both observed mysterious activity that produced clear areas in agar plates otherwise cloudy with thriving bacteria. Something was killing the bacteria. D'Herelle identified the microscopic marvel as a new type of parasite. "In a flash I had understood what caused my clear spots was in fact an invisible microbe . . . a virus parasitic on bacteria," he wrote. He named it bacteriophage, derived from two Greek words and meaning "bacteria devouring."

Early on, phages held much promise in conquering many of the world's scourges. D'Herelle went on to set up an institute with microbiologist George Eliava in Tbilisi, the capital of Georgia. There, they harvested phages from the nearby Kura River for culturing. Though D'Herelle left during the Stalinist era and

Eliava was executed, the Eliava Institute of Bacteriophage, Microbiology, and Virology flourished. In the late 1930s, it churned out phages by the ton. Patients threw back their heads and swallowed a solution of the phages. Several major U.S. pharmaceutical companies—Eli Lilly, for one—entered the field.

But the advent of sulfa drugs and antibiotics in the 1940s relegated phages to the backseat—at least in Western countries. While phages frequently and inexplicably failed, antibiotics, it seemed, were fail-safe. Physicians preferred the new class of drugs because they were relatively easy to use, killed a broad spectrum of bacterial infections, and didn't pose the risk living organisms do.

Later on, because of their structural and genetic simplicity and ease of growth in the lab, Western researchers tapped bacteriophages as model systems to study the molecular basis of genetics, spawning the science of molecular biology. The lab techniques that made the revolution possible were largely advanced through research on phages and their bacterial hosts.

"If you look at the early Nobel Prizes in molecular biology, half of the awards went to researchers using phages," NIMH's Merril says. The work also helped researchers understand the shortcomings of phage therapy of the past. Some of the preparations were contaminated. On top of that, early researchers didn't realize that each phage type is highly specific for a given bacteria species, more finicky than Morris the cat.

Back in the Baltimore lab, Chighladze painstakingly isolates phages from harbor water by culturing them with sundry strains of bacteria. Modern technology can decipher which type of phage kills which type of bacteria. For a broad spectrum assault, purified phages can then be combined in cocktails.

Over time, bacteria naturally develop resistance to phages, as they do to antibiotic drugs. Drug resistance, however, has been accelerated by global misuse of antibiotics. Phages, in contrast, can adapt to keep up with the bacteria, matching their prey mutation for mutation. "It's a biological arms race," explains Sulakvelidze, a former Georgian lab director who worked extensively with the Eliava Institute. Back in Tbilisi, phages never fell out of fashion. They've been in use in humans for 70 years with claims of miraculous results. Phages offer other advantages over antibiotics. For starters, they don't harm benevolent bacteria living in symbiosis with human hosts. But even with such positive traits, phages do have their downside.

Rather than kill bacteria, some phages make them even more lethal. This happens, for example, with the bacterium that causes cholera.

In the mid-1980s interest in the West was renewed when British and Polish researchers studied phage success against microbes in animals. But burgeoning cases of antibiotic-resistant bacterial infections really prompted the surge in Western research.

Today Intralytix and Phage Therapeutics, like a handful of other companies, are developing phage catalogs to sequence the genetic code of a select hundred or so of the inestimably large number of species of bacteria-killing viruses found in nature. Although Intralytix has opted to use only naturally occurring species for now, other companies are attempting to genetically engineer phages so that they overcome bacterial resistance.

The first human clinical trials in the United States are slated to begin within a year. Possible applications include impregnating artificial skin or other materials with phages to heal infected wounds, intravenously medicating patients suffering from bacterial infections of the bloodstream, and culturing custom phage therapies from infected patients.

Psychological barriers to phage acceptance remain. "Some people worry about getting treated with a virus," Merril says, "but they don't realize that many of today's leading vaccines are made with live virus." Yet even Merril doubts phages will ever be a panacea or more than an adjunct to antibiotics.

Whatever the future, phages have already earned a respected place in the annals of medicine. We shall see how much larger their entry becomes.

Reprinted with permission from Julie Wakefield and *Smithsonian Magazine*.

The usefulness of viruses is not only limited to the ability of some to specifically kill bacteria. Over the last few years, viruses have been harnessed for experimental cancer therapies with some success. The key lies in scientists' ability to manipulate viral genomes, by removing genes that allow the virus to cause disease and replacing them with desirable genes. Some

examples that you will see in this article include placing genes that encode toxins into a virus that can target cancer cells or forcing viruses to produce tumor proteins, which sparks an immune response against both the virus and any tumor cells. How do the viruses know to infect only cancer cells? Researchers such as James M. Markert, a neurosurgeon at the University of Alabama at Birmingham, have found that certain types of viruses are attracted to cells showing the misregulation of a protein called ras. The vast majority of cancer cells have this misregulation, while normal body cells do not. This article details the advances that are being made with such viruses by capitalizing on their natural cancer-cell targeting abilities and adding some uniquely human genetic weapons. —JL

"Infectious Notion"
by Ruth Bennett
Science News, August 19, 2000

Poisons. Radiation. Scalpels. Cancer treatments can sound as dangerous as the disease itself. Standard therapies tend to swipe at cells almost indiscriminately, damaging healthy tissue while killing tumors. The lack of specificity can mean even more misery to an already suffering patient.

As candidates for the anticancer toolkit, viruses may seem to belong to the same therapeutic category as poison and radiation. Researchers, however, have new strategies to make viruses into a more compliant instrument.

Whereas traditional cancer treatments blast the disease with a swath of killing power, viruses can provide a fine, deadly beam potentially no wider than a gene and perhaps a substantial improvement in care.

The idea of using viruses as anticancer agents isn't new. The story reaches back nearly a century to doctors who noticed tumor regressions in cancer patients after they contracted viral diseases such as pneumonia. Until recently, however, technical limitations made research into viral treatments sporadic at best.

In one 1956 study, for example, doctors introduced adenovirus into 30 patients with cervical carcinoma. The virus, responsible for the common cold, had been isolated 3 years earlier and was known to kill epithelial cell types that are the first manifestation of most tumors. The experiment succeeded in initially shrinking many tumors, says Steven Linke, a molecular biologist at the National Cancer Institute in Bethesda, Md. However, the tumors returned, and the patients died within less than 3 months.

With the ascendancy of chemotherapy in the 1960s, anticancer viral research retreated. Now, however, as scientists are unlocking the mechanisms that regulate cell division and unraveling the puzzles of infection and immunity, interest in viral treatments for cancer is reemerging.

Latest Direction

The latest direction of research has grown out of gene therapy techniques, which use viruses to deliver genes to living cells, says Edmund C. Lattime, a researcher at the Cancer Institute of New Jersey in New Brunswick. In gene therapy, scientists typically modify viruses so they can't replicate in the patient's body and cause infection.

Early clinical trials of gene therapy to combat genetic disorders weren't particularly impressive, he says. "A lot of us were naive when we started this a number of years ago, thinking we were just going to take viruses . . . and that they were automatically going to do what we wanted them to do," says Lattime.

After struggling with the problems of how to insert genes into huge quantities of cells, and, especially, how to evade immune problems when repeated injections of cells were required, success appeared to be at hand in early 1999. That year, for example, scientists used a modified adenovirus to deliver normal versions of a gene called *p53* to the lung tumors of 25 people. In many cases of cancer, mutations in *p53* stop malignant cells from going into a natural cell-death phase called apoptosis. In 18 of the patients, the injections either reduced or arrested tumor growth.

Scientists have also had success with a related technique called suicide gene therapy. The strategy is to introduce to a tumor site a gene encoding a toxin that can kill cancer cells. The technique also can deliver genes to block the formation of blood vessels feeding the tumor or to activate chemotherapy agents, says Antonio Chiocca, a neurosurgeon at Massachusetts General Hospital in Boston.

However, gene therapy has also had its much-publicized pitfalls.

In 1999, Jesse Gelsinger, an 18-year-old volunteer with a non-life-threatening disease that prevented proper processing of nitrogen, received gene therapy at the University of Pennsylvania in Philadelphia. The goal was to introduce the gene for an enzyme that would control his condition. Instead, he died within 15 days of receiving a high dose of the adenovirus carrying the gene. His death sparked congressional hearings, and the Food and Drug Administration temporarily halted similar gene-therapy trials at other research sites.

Sparked by the limitations of gene therapy, some cancer researchers are now attempting to capitalize on what viruses do best: replicate.

In both traditional and suicide gene therapy techniques, the virus is an inert vehicle that delivers its payload to a tumor. In contrast, cancer researchers are now developing therapies in which injected viruses reproduce and spread throughout the body.

As risky as traditional gene therapy can be, introducing a replicating virus into a patient is fraught with even more danger. Cancer specialists must strike a delicate balance. For safety, the virus must be purified, weakened, and modified. Ideally, it should be nonlethal in its original form, just in case any safeguard fails. It must be innocuous enough to slip past a patient's immune system, but infectious enough to reach all the tumor sites.

What lures the researchers is the possibility of finding or creating a replicating virus that confines its activities to the boundaries of its target tumor and doesn't infect healthy tissue.

Chemotherapy drugs have traditionally had a thera-peutic index of no better than 6 to 1, meaning that they destroy up to 6 cancer cells for every healthy cell that dies. In contrast, one adenovirus currently being developed to fight prostate cancer by Calydon Pharmaceuticals in Sunnyvale, Calif., has demonstrated in animal experiments a therapeutic index of 10,000 to 1.

Replicating Viruses

Work with replicating viruses has had a twofold goal: making agents that boost a patient's immune system and others that directly attack the tumor. Often, the same modified viral genome can be the staging ground for both efforts.

In one immune strategy, researchers use a tradi-tional vaccine approach. Tumors themselves elicit an immune response from the body, but often it's not strong enough to overcome the malignant growth. Viruses manipulated to carry the gene for a tumor protein can boost the immune response. Researchers hope that such strategies will not only destroy an existing tumor but also trigger an immune-system memory that can ward off cancer recurrence.

In other instances, researchers load a virus with genes for proteins called cytokines, chemicals that normally activate elements of the immune system. Once inside the malignant cells, the genes turn the tumor into a cytokine-production mill and make it the agent of its own destruction.

Some of the latest work to exploit the relationship between viruses and the immune system offers the possibility of sidestepping a traditional problem in cancer therapies: getting the viral vehicle to all the sites of malignancy.

In a November 1999 paper in *Human Gene Therapy*, a team led by Robert L. Martuza at Georgetown University Medical Center in Washington, D.C., reported that cancer-ridden mice injected with a strain of herpesvirus experienced tumor regression both at the injection site and in remote growths. Further, they found, remote tumors regressed even at sites that the herpesvirus hadn't reached. The virus appeared to act like a red cape waved before a bull: It directed the immune system's attention to cancer cells, even distant ones, previously ignored.

Finding Viruses

Other strategies focus on finding viruses that will infect and kill cancer cells while leaving healthy cells alone. At least two families of viruses, parvovirus and reovirus, appear to naturally have such selectivity. Scientists also can engineer the property into other viruses, such as poliovirus, herpesvirus, adenovirus, and a candidate currently being tested, a lentivirus derived from HIV.

One way that researchers change viruses into cancer fighters is by taking out the genes that encode enzymes needed for replication. The virus will then grow and kill only in actively dividing cancer cells and others that have a rich supply of those enzymes. Slowly dividing healthy cells are a poor source of enzymes and so aren't affected by the virus.

Some researchers suspect that certain viruses are naturally attracted to cells in which a specific molecular pathway has gone awry. This so-called ras signaling pathway, which controls cell proliferation, differentiation, and death, is abnormally active in most cancer cells, reports Patrick Lee, a virologist at the University of Calgary in Alberta.

"We found that the correlation is amazing," says Lee. "We believe that 80 percent, maybe even more, of all [cancerous] cell lines have an activated *ras* signaling pathway."

In a paper scheduled for publication in the *Proceedings of the National Academy of Sciences*, Lee and his colleagues give evidence that some laboratory-modified herpesviruses infect only cells with *ras* activation. Though the natural herpesvirus can cause meningitis and encephalitis, researchers are able to delete the genes that make the virus dangerous.

James M. Markert, a neurosurgeon at the University of Alabama at Birmingham, works with the HSV-1 strain of herpesvirus. He tries to exploit the virus' natural affinity for the central nervous system by pitting it against neural gliomas. Inaccessible, inoperable, and protected against chemotherapy agents by the blood-brain barrier, these cancers are nearly always fatal. With currently available treatments, half the patients die within a year of diagnosis, and the 5-year survival rate is less than 5.5 percent, says Markert.

An advantage to herpesvirus, says Markert, is that it possesses a large genome, into which researchers can pack more foreign material than other viruses will accommodate. Thus, researchers can try a double-whammy strategy, modifying a single glioma-seeking herpesvirus to carry genes that encode both immune-enhancing cytokines and that deliver suicide instructions to the tumor.

Markert and his colleagues have tried this herpes-plus-immunotherapy technique against gliomas in mice. In a study described in the Feb. 29 *Proceedings of the National Academy of Sciences*, they demonstrated that treated mice survive more than twice as long as untreated animals.

In the May *Gene Therapy*, researchers working with two strains of defanged, modified herpesvirus in the United States and in Scotland reported reassuring results of the first human safety trials in patients with malignant brain tumors. David H. Kirn of the Viral and Genetic Therapy Programme at Hammersmith Hospital in London, hails the safety results as "remarkable" in an editorial accompanying the report.

Researchers weren't studying efficacy in these trials, but their reports of "anecdotal cases of tumor shrinkage or prolonged progression-free intervals were encouraging," says Kirn.

Reserved Enthusiasm

Although Lee helped discover that the herpesvirus targets the *ras* pathway, it's not the virus he champions as an anticancer weapon. Lee's enthusiasm is reserved for the reovirus, which targets the ras pathway even without modification.

The *reo* part of the name is an acronym for respiratory enteric orphan. The orphan designation, says Lee, means that the virus hasn't been linked to any known human disease, very unlike herpesvirus. Lee favors the reovirus because, also unlike herpesvirus, it is extremely easy to grow in large quantities. "What's the advantage of reovirus over herpes?" Lee asks, rhetorically. "Given a choice, which would you pick?"

The choice, however, isn't limited to the herpes and reovirus families. In fact, the workhorse of the field so far, says Lattime, is adenovirus, the same pathogen that yielded such dismal results in the 1950s and the tragedy last year.

The adenovirus has been studied the most and development of treatments that use it are furthest along, Lattime says. Its mechanism for seeking cancer cells is known. A research team led by Frank McCormick, a molecular biologist at the University of California, San Francisco, reported in 1996 that adenovirus targets cancer by identifying cells in which p53 can no longer prevent indiscriminate growth.

The efficacy of adenovirus, particularly when used in conjunction with more traditional chemotherapy, is impressive. In the August *Nature Medicine*, a team headed by Fadlo R. Khuri of the Texas Medical Center in Houston reports that 25 of 30 patients with advanced head and neck cancer responded favorably to a combination of chemotherapy and an adenovirus called ONYX-015. The tumors in eight patients disappeared entirely.

Emerging Therapies

Even with the progress being made with adenovirus, it's likely that several viruses will emerge as cancer therapies, each with its own strengths and weaknesses.

Reovirus isn't the disease threat that herpesvirus is, but researchers can't modify reovirus to evade the immune response, as they have herpesvirus, Chiocca says. In fact, Lattime expresses doubt that cancer patients, scheduled to receive reovirus in the first safety trials this year, will be able to receive multiple injections without developing an immune response against the treatment.

Immunity and the other broad challenges that the scientists face with all viral families can be overcome, Chiocca predicts. Immunosuppressive drugs, carefully administered, may become necessary elements of viral therapy.

The researchers agree that the trend in their field is to try to find the perfect niche for each virus. "I think, based on past experience, that there really isn't any magic bullet for all cancers," says Linke.

Instead, the scientists want to appreciate the idiosyncrasies of each viral strain and each cancer type and find matches between disease and therapy. In the future, Chiocca predicts, "there will be a variety of different viruses with engineered mutations . . . so that each virus will be like a different drug."

Still, one team of geneticists at the University of Alabama at Birmingham cautions in the July *Nature Biotechnology*, "Claims of selective magic bullets need to be modest, though, because much remains to be known about the regulation of viral replication and how to harness it."

Web Sites

Due to the changing nature of Internet links, The Rosen Publishing Group, Inc., has developed an online list of Web sites related to the subject of this book. This site is updated regularly. Please use this link to access the list:

http://www.rosenlinks.com/cdfb/cell

For Further Reading

Becker, Wayne M., Lewis J. Kleinsmith, and Jeff Hardin. *The World of the Cell*. San Francisco, CA: Benjamin Cummings, 2002.

Harold, Franklin M. *The Way of the Cell: Molecules, Organisms and the Order of Life*. New York, NY: Oxford University Press, 2003.

Heller, Craig, David Sadava, Gordon Orians, and William K. Purves. *Life: The Science of Biology*. New York, NY: W. H. Freeman, 2000.

Pollard, Thomas, and William C. Earnshaw. *Cell Biology*. Philadelphia, PA: W. B. Saunders Company, 2002.
Thomas, Lewis. *The Lives of a Cell: Notes of a Biology Watcher*. New York, NY: Penguin Books, 1995.

Bibliography

Alberts, Bruce, Alexander Johnson, Julian Lewis, Martin Raff, Dennis Bray, Karen Hopkin, Keith Roberts, and Peter Walter. *Essential Cell Biology*. New York, NY: Garland Science, 2003.
Alberts, Bruce, Alexander Johnson, Julian Lewis, Martin Raff, Keith Roberts, and Peter Walter. *Molecular Biology of the Cell*. New York, NY: Garland Science, 2002.
Berg, Jeremy, John Tymoczko, and Lubert Stryer. *Biochemistry*. New York, NY: W. H. Freeman and Company, 2002.
Lewin, Benjamin. *Genes VIII*. Englewood Cliffs, NJ: Prentice Hall, 2003.

Index

About the Editor

Jillian L. Lokere is a writer and editor specializing in the life sciences. She holds a master's degree in biology from Harvard University, where she studied cell biology and genetics. Driven by a love of science, her passion is to communicate new discoveries to the public in an engaging way.

Photo Credits

Front Cover: (Top, left inset) © Inmagine.com; (bottom left) © Pixtal/Superstock; (background) © Royalty Free/Corbis; (lower right inset) © SPL/Photoresearchers, Inc. Back Cover: (bottom inset) © Inmagine.com; (top) © Royalty Free/Corbis.

Designer: Geri Fletcher; Series Editor: Joann Jovinelly